The Cases of E-Governance and Development in Korea

The Cases of E-Governance and Development in Korea

Edited by

Dongsung Kong and Moon-Gi Jeong

SKKUP

Table of Contents

Forward

The rapid advancement of Information and Communication Technology (ICT) has continued to shape and reshape the era of the knowledge-based economy. Governments also joined the trend of ICT-based management as a crucial tool for improving not only managerial efficiency but also democratic values, such as responsiveness, citizen participation, and transparency.

While social problems became more complex, a small government ethos with less resources prevailed among citizens. This required that governments provide more services in a somewhat different manner than before. That is, governments should search for new ways of thinking and systems to cope with such challenges. The integration of a government management system and expansion of on-line services through two way communications were considered to be crucial for reducing costs of public service delivery, while increasing responsiveness to the public and government transparency. It eventually required the transformation of traditional ways of identifying citizen demands and delivering public services. E-Government initiatives and the successful implementation of them were expected to upgrade the quality of public services and improve government productibility in the long run, resulting in the enhancement of national competitiveness.

In this vein, countries, whether advanced or developing, have made continuous efforts to devise an e-Government policy and legal framework to establish an e-Government system and to invest and install IT infrastructure. Nevertheless, there still existed big challenges among developing countries regarding political leaders' will and the perception of e-Government initiatives, lack of financial resources for IT infrastructures, technical deficiencies, lack of the public perception of e-Government, and insufficient social infrastructures. Furthermore, developing countries continued to raise concerns about lack of government capacity in the context of experts or professionals in field level officials, who were supposed to play major roles to implement in daily administration.

ADB recognized that lack of government capacity could function as a significant barrier to the realization of e-Government and thus made a policy and technical support for enhancing government capacity in collaboration with the Korean government. Over the last three decades, the Korean government has made continuous efforts to transform government operations and management to be more efficient, responsive and transparent through the establishment of an e-Government system. It led Korea to become a world leader in e-Government, recently achieving first rank among all UN member countries in 2012 UN e-Government. As a consequence, many countries attempted to benchmark and learn Korea's approaches and experiences for e-Government and strategies for better adoption and implementation in their countries. Korea should respond to increasing demands by sharing its experiences and know-how with other countries.

With this background, the case studies in this book are aimed at sharing Korea's useful experiences and know-how with other countries, especially developing countries that intended to adopt more efficient and responsive government system by enhancing e-Government capacity. Recognizing the significance of e-Government capacity in developing countries, Korea government and ADB initiated joint consulting through 'Supporting Public Management through e-Government Capacity Development' in 2012. Several experts or professionals from academics and public offices joined in these case studies by contributing their research and practical experiences gained in the process of formulating and implementing economic development and e-Government policy in Korea. The authors prepared a report dealing with Korean experiences of e-Government systems. Based on the report, the authors made extensive revisions and expansions to update and provide broader aspects and contexts of e-Government policies and governance. Furthermore, they added two chapters including 'Financing economic development in Korea' and 'Local information villages in Korea'.

With regard to knowledge sharing of Korean e-Government systems, the book contains case studies covering diverse aspects of e-governance and development and consists of eight chapters.

Chapter 1 discusses the role of the Korean government for economic development, focusing on financial efforts and policies. It provides the historical evolution of economic development since the era of foreign aid in 1945 and the general context of the transformation into an ICT-centered e-Government system in Korea.

With this background, Chapter 2 provides overarching pictures of the e-Government of Korea focusing an institutions, policies, and laws. The chapter addresses a historical context of e-Government since the mid-1980s, which shows incremental steps taken by the Korean government. In doing so, it emphasizes strong leadership and a well-organized design of e-Government related policies for the success of e-Government.

Chapter 3 explores the case of eProcurement in Korea. In 2001, the Korean government established the Korean ON-line E-Procurement System (KONEPS) to streamline and achieve efficiency and transparency of procurement processes. Nevertheless, as it experienced continuous challenges of the standards and expansion of customers including small and medium-size enterprises, and female-owned and socially disadvantaged people's enterprises, the chapter asserts that the eProcurement system should continue to improve legal and technical measures.

Chapter 4 deals with the Tax Administration Information System (TAMIS) in Korea. It indicates that the Korean government followed step-by-step phases to install TMIS between 1967 and 2006, showing processes of trials-and errors. It might provide useful insights for those countries planning to initiate TAMIS. In doing so, the chapter places special emphasis on human factors including internal tax officials and external tax payers.

On the other hand, Chapter 5 discusses the specific topic of the Value Added Tax (VAT) invoice system. It has more significance in developing countries due to a very narrow VAT tax base and the challenges of compliance costs. After it delineates significance, concepts, and necessary conditions for the electronic VAT invoicing system, it lays out three dimensions to optimize the electronic VAT invoicing system: accessibility, easy use of system, and personalization.

Chapter 6 introduces the Social Welfare Integrated Management Network (SWIMN) in Korea. Since many Asian-Pacific countries experienced poverty, income gaps, and high unemployment, social safety net or social welfare programs have gained greater attention among the public and government. In doing so, the chapter underlines a seamless and integrated social welfare information system. In Korea, the SWIMN played a crucial role for effective and efficient delivery of social welfare services.

Chapter 7 discusses the National Health Information System (NHIS) in Korea. Since the current society experienced rapid growth of the aging population and an increasing rate of chronic diseases, countries, whether developed or developing, should take active roles and make new initiatives in health related administration. The chapter introduces the NHIS in Korea emphasizing the significance of the initial master plan, clear vision, and the institutional and legal frames. Furthermore, it continues to elaborate on the coordination issues of about 3,500 public health institutions. However, it recognizes that some challenges are still far ahead including stakeholder involvements and the formation of a robust conceptual framework.

The final chapter deals with information villages in Korea. While the previous chapters primarily focus on the e-Government and governance at the national level, this chapter focuses on local informatization efforts to bridge the digital divide and improve the living standards at the local level. It provides insight into setting up local information villages and the consequences of informatization on local development.

We are grateful to Kyu-Myoung Lee and Seong-ho Park for their help in the preparation of this book. We would like to note that this work was supported by the National Research Foundation of Korea Grant funded by the Korean Government (NRF-2013S1A3A2055108).

Dongsung Kong and Moon-Gi Jeong

May 2015

Chapter 1

Financing South Korea's Economic Development

Dongsung Kong (Sungkyunkwan University)

Financing South Korea's Economic Development

Dongsung Kong (Sungkyunkwan University)

1. Introduction

In the early years after the Independence of Korea (1945), the South Korean government was heavily dependent on foreign aid, mostly from the United States. The country's already miserable economy and public finances were further aggravated by the Korean War (1950-1953). Despite all the hardships, South Korea started to develop its economy from the ashes, and managed to accelerate its high growth for decades. In 1996, South Korea joined the OECD (Organization for Economic Cooperation and Development), and increased its financial contributions to developing countries. In 2008, sixty years after the establishment of the Republic of Korea, the country became part of the G-20 leadership. As shown in Figure 1-1, South Korea's per capita GNI has soared by approximately 500 times since gaining independence from Japanese colonialism (1910-1945).

What made this remarkable achievement, which was often praised as a miracle ("the Miracle on the Han River"), possible? Was there any secret formula for this success? Many agree that former president Park Chung-hee, who executed four 'Five-Year Economic Development Plans' successfully, was one of the most important contributors to this miracle. At the same time, many also argue that it was the general public who worked so hard supporting the labor-intensive industrialization and sacrificed themselves for prolonged aggressive investment in education for the future generations. And the role of the private sector, particularly firms and conglomerates, in the export-driven economic development strategy, was also very crucial in the whole course of South Korea's economic development. Indeed, it was the result of concerted efforts among the government, the private sector, and the people.

"The South Korean experience contradicts the 'Washington consensus,' which is opposed to government-led development and has tied the hands of policy makers in most developing countries. South Korean development was led by an activist government – mobilising private entrepreneurs, the bureaucracy and the general public – that pushed its plan for economic growth and gave continual detailed attention to economic matters" (Adelman, 1999: 57-58). Adelman argues that "had the neoliberal prescriptions forced on most LDCs [Least Developed Countries] been adopted in South Korea during the 1960s and 1970s, there would not have been a South Korean economic miracle (1999: 58)."

This Chapter highlights the role of the Korean government for economic development. It claims that active governance equipped with good governing strategies and economic policies is one of the most critical reasons why South Korea managed to turn around from the war-torn economy and continued its economic growth for decades. To better illustrate South Korea's governing strategies by developmental stages, this chapter divides the country's economic development chronology into four as shown in Box 1. This Chapter analyses the country's political & social context, economic conditions, governing strategies and economic policies, and performance particularly during the first three eras.

Box 1. South Korea's Economic Development Stages

The Era of Foreign Aid (1945 – 1961)

The Era of Economic Development (1961 – 1979)

The Era of Stabilization & Globalization (1979 – 1997)

The Era of Post-Development (1998 – Present)

Figure 1-1. Per Capita GNI: South Korea, 1945-2013

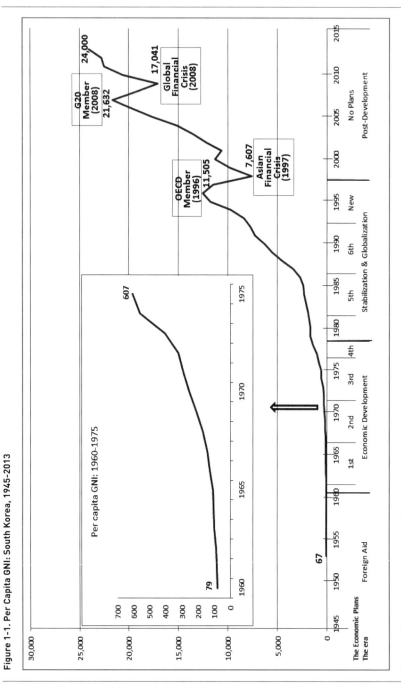

*Source: The Bank of Korea. Economic Statistics System.

**Note: The figures during 1953-1969 are based on Per Capita GNP. The figure for 2013 is estimated.

2. The Era of Foreign Aid (1945-1961)

1) Political & Social Context

With the end of the Japanese occupation of Korea (1910–1945), the Korean peninsular was divided into two Koreas: the North administered by the Soviet Union and the South by the United States. The modern history of South Korea formally begins with its establishment on August 15, 1948, the First Republic, with Rhee Syngman as the first president. In a few years, the Korean peninsular turned into a bombarding battlefield (1950-1953). After the armistice in 1953, South Korea experienced political turmoil mainly due to election corruptions and autocratic ruling of the first president Rhee Syngman, who had to resign from office foilowing a student revolt in 1960. The Democratic Party gained power and the Second Republic was established in August, 1960. But even with the new government political turmoil was not alleviated and perhaps even worsened, and the May 16 coup, led by Major General Park Chung-hee, ended the Second Republic in 1961.

2) Economic Conditions

The economy of South Korea during 1945–1961 was in dire condition. Savada & Shaw (1992) succinctly summarizes South Korea's economic situation which was not just miserable but also disadvantaged compared with North Korea, as described in Box 2.

Box 2. South Korea Under United States Occupation: 1945-48

(Savada and Shaw, 1992: 29)

The division of Korea into two zones at an arbitrary line further aggravated the situation. There were many inherent problems in building a self-sufficient economy in the southern half of the peninsula. Most of the heavy industrial facilities were located in northern Korea -- the Soviet zone -- including the chemical plants that produced necessary agricultural fertilizers. Light industries in southern Korea had been dependent on electricity from the hydraulic generators located on the Yalu River on the Korean-Manchurian border; electric generating facilities in the south supplied only 9 percent of the total need. Railroads and industries in the south also had been dependent upon bituminous coal imported from Manchuria, Japan, and the north (although the south had been exporting some excess anthracite to the north).

The problems were compounded by the fact that most of Korea's mines and industries had been owned and operated by Japan. As the United States military government let the 700,000 Japanese depart from South Korea in the months following the start of the American occupation, almost all of the mines and factories - now enemy properties vested in the military government - were without managers, technicians, and capital resources. This situation led to severe unemployment and material shortages.

3) Governing Strategies and Economic Policy

During the period of 1945-1961, there was no effectively implemented economic policy or strategy. The country's economy and its public finances were heavily dependent on foreign aid, mostly coming from the United States. Vaughn Mechau (1961: 1), who was the secretary general of the Combined Economic Board, summarizes in his report that "from 1945 to 1960 (FY '61) the United States Government extended to the Republic of Korea for economic assistance, (excluding military assistance), total funds in excess of $3,194,639,000." The portion between 1945 and 1954 was $1,000,000,000; and $2,194,639,000 between 1954 and 1960 (Mechau, 1961: 1). The former minister of Finance and Economy, Kang Kyung-Sik (Jaikyunghoi-Yewoohoi, 2011: 40), witnesses that "A counterpart fund had been the main financial resource of the country's public finance until the National Tax Service was created in 1966. A counterpart fund was a way for turning foreign aid (materials) into reserves of domestic currency. At those times, we had no meaningful public finance without foreign aid."

Box 3. The Postwar Economy

(Savada and Shaw, 1992: 36)

The war had destroyed most of South Korea's production facilities. The South Korean government began rehabilitation as soon as the battle zone near the thirty-eighth parallel stabilized in 1952. The United Nations Korean Reconstruction Agency and members of the UN, principally the United States, also provided badly needed financial assistance. Seoul depended

---

heavily on foreign aid, not only for defense, but also for other expenditures. Foreign aid constituted a third of the total budget in 1954, rose to 58.4 percent in 1956, and was approximately 38 percent of the budget in 1960. The first annual United States economic aid bill after the armistice was US$200 million; aid peaked at US$365 million in 1956 and was then maintained at the US$200 million level annually until the mid-1960s.

Table 1-1. The Sources of Foreign Aid: 1945-1965

(Unit: Millions of US$)

Year	GARIOA	ECA&SEC	PL480	ICA&AID	CRIK	UNKRA	Total
1945	4.9						4.9
1946	49.5						49.5
1947	175.4						175.4
1948	179.6						179.6
1949	92.7	23.8					116.5
1950		49.3			9.4		58.7
1951		31.9			74.5	0.1	106.5
1952		3.8			155.5	1.9	161.3
1953		0.2		5.6	158.8	29.6	194.2
1954				82.4	50.2	21.3	153.9
1955				205.8	8.7	22.2	236.7
1956			33.0	271.1	0.3	22.4	326.7
1957			45.5	323.3		14.1	382.9
1958			47.9	265.6		7.8	321.3
1959			11.4	208.3		2.7	222.5
1960			19.9	225.2		0.2	245.4

1961			44.9	156.6			201.6
1962			67.3	165.0			232.3
1963			96.8	119.7			216.5
1964			61.0	88.4			149.3
1965			59.5	71.9			131.4
Total	502.1	109.2	487.3	2,188.8	457.4	122.35	3,867.1

*Source: The Bank of Korea. Economic Statistics Yearbook, 1960-1966.
**Note: GARIOA(Government Appropriation for Relief in Occupied Areas).
ECA(Economic Cooperation Administration).
SEC(Supplies for Economic Cooperation).
PL480(Public law 480, Agricultural Trade Development & Assistance Act).
ICA(International Cooperation Administration).
CRIK(Civil Relief in Korea).
UNKRA(United Nations Korea Reconstruction Agency).
*CRIK and UNKRA were under the name of U.N. But the most portion of the funds was contributed by the United States.

3. The Era of Economic Development (1961–1979)

1) Political & Social Context

Through a military coup (May 16, 1961), Park Chung-hee seized power, and ruled the country as the head of the Supreme Council for National Reconstruction. In 1963 he was officially elected as the President of the Third Republic (1963-1971). In 1971, Park won a third term after amending the Constitution that had limited presidents to two terms, and became president for life, the Fourth Republic (1972-1979), until he was assassinated in 1979.

Box 4. Park Chung-hee

(Encyclopaedia Britannica)

Born into an impoverished rural family, Park graduated (1937) with top honours from Taegu (Daegu) Normal School, after which he taught primary school. After attending a Japanese military academy, Park served as a second lieutenant in the Japanese army during World War II and became an officer in the Korean army when Korea was freed from Japanese rule after the war. He was made a brigadier general (1953) during the Korean War (1950–53) and was promoted to general in 1958. On May 16, 1961, he led a military coup that overthrew the Second Republic. He remained the leader of the junta until two years later, when he won the first of his three terms as president of the Third Republic.

At home Park maintained a policy of guided democracy, with restrictions on personal freedoms, suppression of the press and of opposition parties, and control over the judicial system and the universities. He organized and expanded the Korean Central Intelligence Agency (KCIA; now the National Intelligence Service), which became a much-feared agent of political repression. Park claimed that all his measures were necessary to fight communism. In foreign affairs, he continued the close relations his predecessors Syngman Rhee and Yun Po Sŏn had maintained with the United States. Park was responsible in large part for South Korea's "economic miracle"; the programs he initiated gave his country one of the fastest-growing economies in the world.

On Oct. 17, 1972, Park declared martial law, and one month later he installed a repressive authoritarian regime, the Yushin ("Revitalization Reform") order, with a new constitution that gave him sweeping powers. He grew increasingly harsh toward political dissidents. After Park's dismissal (1979) of popular opposition leader Kim Young Sam from the National Assembly, Korea erupted with severe riots and demonstrations. Park was assassinated by his lifelong friend Kim Jae Kyu, the head of the KCIA.

2) Economic Conditions

The economic conditions of the early 1960s were still miserable. "Foreign aid and government loans to an impoverished South Korea were financing more than half of imports and over 80 percent of investment" (Adelman, 1999: 58). The Figure 1-2 illustrates the situation of the early 1960s of South Korea in the format of a SWOT (Strengths, Weaknesses, Opportunities, and Threats) analysis.

Figure 1-2. A SWOT Analysis of South Korea in the early 1960s

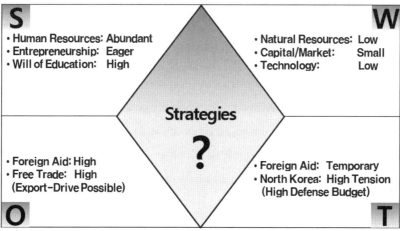

3) Governing Strategies and Economic Policy

The main governing goal of the Third Republic was building a self-sustaining economy as soon as possible. The meaning of self-sustaining economy to the policy-makers of the Third Republic of Korea was creating and maintaining a good relationship between public finance and the market economy. In other words, good public finance promotes the market economy, and the good market economy in return expands the tax base for public finance: and this virtuous cycle repeats, as illustrated in Figure 1-3.

Figure 1-3. A virtuous Circle of Public Finance and the Economy

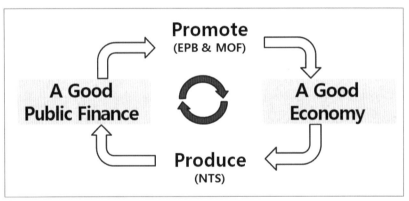

The challenge was 'who should go first' when neither the government nor the private sector had sufficient resources to prime the pump in the South Korea of the early 1960s. The answer to this challenge in the Third Republic was a centrally-managed economy as a way to concentrate all the available resources on economic development. The operational strategies for achieving the self-sustaining economy can be summarized as follows:

(1) Governing Structure for Economic Development

The first step for economic development was having the right organizational set-up to plan, execute, monitor, and assess the economic activities and performance round by round. The Economic Planning Board (EPB) was created in 1961 as the primary organization to orchestrate all the economic planning matters. Thus, the EPB became the most powerful control-tower in allocating the government budget, securing foreign loans, and designing the five-year economic development plans. Later the National Tax Service (NTS) was created in 1966 to improve the efficiency of tax collection. By setting up EPB and NTS along with the Ministry of Finance which were established in 1948, the structural scheme for creating a virtuous cycle between public finance and the market economy was completed.

(2) Five-Year Economic Development Plans (1962-1981)

The Five-Year Economic Development Plan was a mid-term scheme to achieve the governing goal of the Third Republic, building a self-sustaining economy. Given the economic conditions in the early 1960s, it appeared that the direction and strategies to be employed in the take-off stage (1962-1971) were quite logical as summarized below:

① Promoting the 'Labor–intensive' Industrialization
Given that the country had no sufficient natural resources or competitive technology, the only viable option left for economic development was the full utilization of abundant labor. The Korean government expanded labor-intensive programs, such as construction of new infrastructure (roads, dams, irrigation, etc). This was a win-win strategy to improve employment imme-

diately and equip the workers with higher technology to be competitive in the world marker later on.

② Promoting the 'Export–driven' Industrialization

Given that the domestic market was so small, the best strategy to expand its economic growth was increasing exports. The Korean government concentrated its financial support on the light industry (wigs, garments, shoes, etc.), mostly exporting firms, that could be competitive with low prices in the world market utilizing abundant, cheap, but very diligent labor.

③ Promoting the 'Buy Domestic Products' Movement

Along with the export-driven industrialization, it was also critical to have domestic products protected in the domestic market. Otherwise the gains from exports would be cancelled out by imports. The 'Buy Domestic Products' strategy, which was supported by the general public, was an effective one since infant domestic firms needed time to grow.

④ Establishing Public Corporations

Given that the private entrepreneurs lacked the capital and experience, it was necessary for the government to establish public enterprises, particularly for highly strategic industries, such as utilities, banking, communications, and in some areas of manufacturing.

⑤ Mobilization of Foreign Capital

Foreign aid was essential to the country's recovery from the Korean War (1950-1953) and to economic growth in the 1960s. As the level of foreign aid mostly from the United States, decreased, the country had to find a way to finance the Five-Year Economic Development Plans which required enormous amounts of capital. Mobilizing financial resources was the most challenging task when the size of the domestic economy is so minimal. The Park regime came up with a long-term scheme to mobilize both external and internal financial sources. Given that neither the government nor the private sector had sufficient capital, the Korean government took the initiative in mobilizing financial resources overseas, such as Japan, Germany, and the international capital market. The funds were selectively distributed to the export-driven firms and related government programs.

Box 5. Aid, Loans, and Investment

(Savada and Shaw, 1992: 43-44, 184)

As the level of United States assistance had stabilized, the Park regime turned to "financial diplomacy" with other countries. The normalization of relations with Japan in 1965 brought Japanese funds in the form of loans and compensation for the damages suffered during the colonial era. Park made a state visit to the Federal Republic of Germany in 1964 that resulted in the extension of government aid and commercial credits. The availability of funds and the increasing level of exports elevated Seoul's credit rating, making it possible to increase borrowing in the open international market. Further, the conflict in Indochina stimulated economic growth. Seoul's export drive also owed much to the availability of an educated labor force and a favorable international market.

South Korea became increasingly integrated into the international capital market; from the late 1960s to the mid- 1980s, development was financed

---

with a series of foreign loans, two-thirds of which came from private banks and suppliers' credits. The total external debt grew to a high of US$46.7 billion in 1985. Positive trade balances in the late 1980s led to a rapid decline in foreign debt--from US$35.6 billion in 1987 to an expected US$23 billion by 1991. Account surpluses in 1990 were expected to enable Seoul to reduce its foreign debt from its 1987 level of about 28 percent of GNP to about 10 percent by 1991.

Table 1-2. Foreign Aid and Loans: 1945-1992

(Unit: Millions of US$)

	Foreign Aid		Foreign Loans							Total
			Public Loans		Private Loans1)		Sub-Total			
1945 -1961	3,133.4	(99.5)	15	(0.5)			15	(0.5)		3,148.4
1962	239.3	(78.6)	59	(19.4)	6	(2.0)	65	(21.4)		304.3
1963	216.4	(75.6)	9	(3.1)	61	(21.3)	70	(24.4)		286.4
1964	149.3	(59.9)	36	(14.4)	64	(25.7)	100	(40.1)		249.3
1965	131.4	(42.6)	77	(25.0)	100	(32.4)	177	(57.4)		308.4
1966	103.3	(27.3)	154	(40.7)	121	(32.0)	275	(72.7)		378.3
1967	97.0	(27.0)	88	(24.5)	174	(48.5)	262	(73.0)		359.0
1968	105.9	(14.7)	83	(11.5)	532	(73.8)	615	(85.3)		720.9
1969	107.3	(10.3)	236	(22.6)	703	(67.2)	939	(89.7)		1,046.3
1970	82.6	(12.8)	149	(23.0)	415	(64.2)	564	(87.2)		646.6
1971	51.2	(5.5)	399	(43.1)	476	(51.4)	875	(94.5)		926.2
1972	5.1	(0.5)	551	(56.4)	421	(43.1)	972	(99.5)		977.1
1973	2.1	(0.1)	631	(40.1)	942	(59.8)	1,573	(99.9)		1,575.1
1974	1.0	(0.1)	415	(23.3)	1,367	(76.7)	1,782	(99.9)		1,783.0
1975	1.2	(0.1)	597	(44.0)	759	(55.9)	1,356	(99.9)		1,357.2
1976	1.7	(0.0)	1,378	(38.4)	2,210	(61.6)	3,588	(100.0)		3,589.7

1977	0.9	(0.0)	1,016	(36.9)	1,738	(63.1)	2,754	(100.0)	2,754.9
1978	0.2	(0.0)	2,531	(50.5)	2,483	(49.5)	5,014	(100.0)	5,014.2
1979	0.2	(0.0)	901	(25.7)	2,598	(74.2)	3,499	(100.0)	3,499.2
1980	0.4	(0.0)	2,453	(47.4)	2,717	(52.5)	5,170	(100.0)	5,170.4
1981	0.2	(0.0)	2,443	(45.9)	2,884	(54.1)	5,327	(100.0)	5,327.2
1982	0.1	(0.0)	1,397	(31.5)	3,033	(68.5)	4,430	(100.0)	4,430.1
1983			1,690	(36.7)	2,912	(63.3)	4,602	(100.0)	4,602.0
1984			848	(14.6)	4,943	(85.4)	5,791	(100.0)	5,791.0
1985			741	(10.8)	6,151	(89.2)	6,892	(100.0)	6,892.0
1986			826	(20.5)	3,195	(79.5)	4,021	(100.0)	4,021.0
1987			562	(18.3)	2,503	(81.7)	3,065	(100.0)	3,065.0
1988			520	(19.6)	2,137	(80.4)	2,657	(100.0)	2,657.0
1989			188	(9.5)	1,791	(90.5)	1,979	(100.0)	1,979.0
1990			332	(9.7)	3,097	(90.3)	3,429	(100.0)	3,429.0
1991			942	(11.1)	7,525	(88.9)	8,467	(100.0)	8,467.0
1992			220	(3.9)	5,400	(96.1)	5,620	(100.0)	5,620.0
Sum	4,430.2	(4.9)	22,487	(24.9)	63,458	(70.2)	85,945	(95.1)	90,375.2

*Source:Reorganized from the sources including the Ministry of Finance, the Economic Planning Board, the Bank of Korea, and the Korea Development Bank.

**Notes: 1) Private loans include commercial loans, bonds by financial institutions and private firms, and Foreign Direct Investment (FDI).

2) ( ) refers to the percentage of the total.

⑥ Investing in Education

The only and the best strategy to maintain economic growth in the long term was investing in education which would prepare for the next-stage of industrialization, and become more competitive in the world market.

⑦ Timely Transition of Industrial Policy

It was also important to re-direct the priority industry in a timely manner when the economy was heavily dependent on exports. The Korean government's priorities can be grouped into four stages as summarized below:

▽ Initial Industrialization Stage (1962-1973)

▽ Heavy and Chemical Industry Stage (1973-1979)

▽ Liberalization Stage (1979-1997)

▽ ICT Industrialization Stage (1998-2012)

⑧ Government Control of the Financial Sector

The government decided to control the financial sector to allocate the funds to the industries that the government planned to promote: mostly export-driven industries. In this way the government was able to harmonize its own fiscal policies and the financial sector's monetary policies in a timely manner.

The Korean government incorporated the above strategies stage by stage into Five-Year Economic Development Plans, and was in the forefront of creating opportunities and getting things done. The strategies were executed successfully because the general public and the firms corresponded with enormous enthusiasm. The approach was simple, pragmatic and indeed effective.

Table 1-3. Goals of the Five-Year Economic Development Plans: 1st through 4th

	Goals	Strategic Objectives 1)
First (1962-1966)	Building Self-sustaining Economy	Enhancing Agricultural Production Securing Energy Resources Expanding Core Industry and S.O.C. Export Growth & Improvement of Balance of Payment Enhancement of Technology

Second (1967-1971)	Accelerating Self-sustaining Economy	Development of Food, Forest, & Fisheries Promotion of Chemical, Steel & Machine Industry Export Growth & Improvement of Balance of Payment Enhancement of Science & Management
Third (1972-1976)	Balancing Growth, Stabilization, and Regional Development	Innovative Development of Food, Forest, & Fisheries Acceleration of Exports Acceleration of Heavy & Chemical Industry
Fourth (1977-1981)	Growth, Equity, and Efficiency	Achievement of Self-sustaining Economy Promotion of Social Equity & Environment Technology Innovation & Efficiency

*Source: Economic Planning Board, 1982.
**Note: 1) The strategic objectives listed in the table are the selection of the main ones.

(3) Economic Policies

Since the government controlled the financial sector it was relatively easy to implement its own fiscal and monetary policies. Economic policies were consistent with the main governing goal, building a sustainable economy. the main economic policies are summarized below:

① Preferential Treatment/Incentives for Private Entrepreneurs
The Park regime provided powerful incentives to the businesses that cooperated with the government direction. The incentives included low-interest loans, permission to borrow from the international market, permission to import, tax benefits, etc. The businesses that received these incentives responded with high growth rates, and some of them continued to expand today, such as Samsung, Hyundai, and Posco.

② Government Control of Exchange Rates

Since the country had been suffering from high inflation, the stabilization of exchange rates (mostly devaluation policy) contributed to stabilizing and promoting exports.

③ Promoting Domestic Savings

In the early 1960s, the private financial sector was very unfriendly to businesses and savings. The savings rate as the share of GDP was minimal, ranging only 1-2%, and the interest rates were very high in the private money market. Thus, the government decided to increase the interest rates for savings to promote domestic savings that would be an important source of domestic investment later on.

Box 6. Financing Development

(Savada and Shaw, 1992: 153)

Domestic savings were very low before the mid-1960s, equivalent to less than 2 percent of GNP in the 1960 to 1962 period. The savings rate jumped to 10 percent between 1970 and 1972 when banks began offering depositors rates of 20 percent or more on savings accounts. This situation allowed banks to compete effectively for deposits with unorganized money markets that had previously offered higher rates than the banks. The savings rate increased to 16.8 percent of GNP in 1975 and 28 percent in 1979, but temporarily plunged to 20.8 percent in 1980 because of the oil price rise.

---

4) Performance

South Korea's economy grew rapidly during the period of the first and second Five-Year Economic Development Plan, as shown in Table 1-4. Exports, domestic savings, employment and many other economic indicators were improved dramatically during this period. This success was very meaningful particularly because it provided the firm ground for a self-sustaining economy. In other words, the good relationship between public finance and the market economy was further strengthened and repeated for decades. The rapidly growing economy contributed to rapid increases in government revenues, and the government improved its own capacity for fueling the market economy, as demonstrated in Table 1-5. However, the country was severely threatened by oil crises in 1973 and 1979, because South Korea depended heavily on imported oil. But Seoul managed to overcome these crises through construction contracts in the Middle East, and thus prolonged the high rate of economic growth. The Korean government certainly achieved its governing goal, building a self-sustainable economy, in only 10 years, and was very confident in its future.

Box 7. Economic Development
(Savada and Shaw, 1992: 44)

Substantial successes were achieved under the first two five-year economic development plans. The manufacturing sector provided the main stimulus, growing by 15 percent and 21 percent, respectively, during the two plans. Domestic savings rates grew and exports expanded significantly. A new eco-

---

nomic strategy emphasizing diversification in production and trade proved generally successful in the 1970s. Under the third plan, the government made a bold move to expand South Korea's heavy and chemical industries, investing in steel, machinery, shipbuilding, electronics, chemicals, and non-ferrous metals. South Korea's capability for steel production and oil refining rose most notably. Refineries for zinc and copper and modern shipbuilding facilities were constructed; automobiles began to be exported to a few markets. The plan sought to better prepare South Korea for competition in the world market and to facilitate domestic production of weaponry.

Table 1- 4. The Performance of the Five-Year Economic Development Plans: 1st through 4th

(Unit: Annual Average Percentage)

	GNP Growth		Investment		Domestic savings		Consumer price		Unemployment		Export Growth[2]		Import Growth[2]	
	Plan[1]	Result	Plan	Result	Plan	Result	Plan	Result	Plan	Result	Plan	Result	Plan	Result
First (1962-1966)	7.1	8.5	22.6	15.1	9.2	6.1	-	19.7	8.5	7.6	28.0	38.6	8.7	18.7
Second (1967-1971)	7.0	11.4	19.0	30.6	11.6	15.5	-	15.0	6.1	5.0	17.1	33.8	6.5	25.8
Third (1972-1976)	8.6	10.1	24.9	25.5	21.5	23.1	-	15.9	4.2	4.1	22.7	32.7	13.7	12.6
Fourth (1977-1981)	9.2	5.5	26.0	31.2	26.1	22.3	-	18.6	4.0	4.1	16.0	11.1	12.0	10.5

*Source: Reorganized from the sources including Jaikyunghoi-Yewoohoi, 2011: p.115; Kang, 2000: 44; and the National Archives of Korea.
**Note: 1) The figures are based on the original targets, not the ones revised during the plan.
2) The export/import figures are based on the arrival of commodities.

Box 8. Revenues and Expenditures

(Savada and Shaw, 1992: 145-146)

The central government budget has generally expanded, both in real terms and as a proportion of real GNP, since the end of the Korean War, stabilizing at between 20 and 21 percent of GNP during most of the 1980s. Government spending in South Korea has been less than that for most countries in the world (excepting the other rapidly growing Asian economies of Japan, Taiwan, and Singapore). The share of government spending devoted to investment and other capital formation activities increased steadily through the periods of the first and second five-year plans (1962-1971), peaking at more than 41 percent of the budget in 1969. Since 1971 investment expenditures have remained at less than 30 percent of the budget, while the share of the budget occupied by direct government consumption and transfer payments has continued to increase, averaging more than 70 percent during the 1980s.

Table 1-5. Government Revenues: 1962-1979

(Unit: Millions of Won)

	Taxes		Foreign Aid		Foreign Loans		Total[1]
1962	26,024	(16%)	32,521	(20%)	-	(0%)	161,959
1963	31,079	(18%)	26,312	(15%)	-	(0%)	173,363
1964	37,421	(20%)	28,020	(15%)	-	(0%)	183,713
1965	54,634	(25%)	36,090	(16%)	-	(0%)	222,559
1966	87,646	(25%)	43,837	(13%)	3,580	(1%)	348,056
1967	129,242	(29%)	45,680	(10%)	5,551	(1%)	439,828
1968	194,288	(33%)	39,647	(7%)	5,876	(1%)	589,880

1969	262,823	(31%)	34,385	(4%)	35,211	(4%)	849,453
1970	334,723	(38%)	28,301	(3%)	34,052	(4%)	887,955
1971	407,684	(40%)	21,497	(2%)	51,666	(5%)	1,011,603
1972	433,446	(33%)	27,839	(2%)	97,488	(7%)	1,306,732
1973	521,492	(38%)	22,033	(2%)	80,336	(6%)	1,376,285
1974	844,674	(42%)	23,434	(1%)	53,035	(3%)	1,993,039
1975	1,255,479	(39%)	28,923	(1%)	171,630	(5%)	3,196,890
1976	1,914,747	(44%)	16,340	(0%)	186,867	(4%)	4,392,341
1977	2,402,682	(49%)	12,661	(0%)	185,798	(4%)	4,927,033
1978	3,372,262	(53%)	15,566	(0%)	194,981	(3%)	6,416,507
1979	4,401,708	(52%)	17,885	(0%)	274,469	(3%)	8,540,737
Sum	16,712,053	(45%)	500,970	(1%)	1,380,541	(4%)	37,017,931

*Source: Ministry of Strategy and Finance, Summary of Financial Implementation, 1962-1979.
**Note: 1) The sum of the three categories does not equal to the total because other categories are not included in the table, and some internal transactions between general and special accounts are not factored out.

4. The Era of Stabilization and Globalization (1979–1997)

1) Political & Social Context

President Park, who had framed and operated the economic growth machine for 18 years, was assassinated on October 26, 1979. Not surprisingly, the suppressed voices for democracy erupted all over the country. But another authoritarian ruler, Major General Chun Doo-whan, seized power and ruled the country until 1987. During the Chun regime, the country experienced severe student demonstrations and social turmoil. And, more importantly, the general public were becoming more sympathetic to the student demonstrations. As a result, in the 1985 National Assembly elections, the ruling party was defeated. But the best chance to have a civilian president was blown away by the marginal victory (36.6 percent of votes) of another military ruler, Roh Tae-woo, Chun's long-term colleague, since two opposition party candidates split the votes: 28 and 27.1 percent (National Archives of Korea). However, because President Roh's unpopularity, he had to gradually absorb the demands for democracy. Finally, on December 18, 1992, South Korea elected their first civilian president, Kim Young-sam.

2) Economic Conditions

Mainly due to the oil crisis in 1979, the country suffered a negative growth rate of 4.8% in 1980. In addition, "the new regime inherited an economy suffering from all the side effects of Park's export-oriented development program and his policy of expanding heavy and chemical industries. The international economic environment of the early 1980s was extremely unfavorable, a situation that further restricted South Korea's exports" (Savada and Shaw, 1992: 59).

3) Governing Strategies and Economic Policy

The Chun & Roh regimes maintained most of the governing strategies and economic policies of the Park regime, but they had to adjust some of them to correct the side effects of the Park's programs and to respond to new challenges. The main theme of the revision was 'stabilization and liberalization' in order to adapt to the less friendly trend in the trade market and domestically embrace the needs of democratization and social equity. The main governing strategies and economic policies included ① more emphasis on inflation control, ② diversification of products and services, ③ more emphasis on fair trade, ④ more emphasis on R&D, and ⑤ more autonomy of the private sector.

Box 9. Stabilization and Liberalization Policies

(Heo, 2001: 225-226)

In April of 1979, the Korean government announced the Comprehensive Stabilization Program (CSP). The major contents of the CSP included: 1) scaling back the role of policy targeting in the operation of preferential policy loans and interest rates; 2) increasing the trade liberalization ratio from 69% in 1986 to 95% in 1988; 3) stressing on the promotion of technology investment from 0.9% of GNP in 1980 to 2% in 1986 and 2.5% by 1990. The Technology Development Promotion Act, which was originally enacted in 1973, was strengthened in 1981 to provide new tax incentives for R&D investment.

Government continued to take an aggressive role ... It restructured the machinery industry by merging major heavy electrical equipment producers (Hyosung, Kolong, and Ssangyong) in 1980 and assigned them monopoly status. Hyundai International's Changwon complex (renamed KHIC in 1980 under KEPCO management) was nationalized and split into components under the management of Samsung, LG, and KEPCO in 1983. A shipping industry rationalization plan was initiated, resulting in a decrease in the number of companies from 60 to about 15 (World Bank 1987).

A Fair Trade Law was adopted in 1981 to guard domestic fair trade practices against anti-competitive mergers as well as restrictive trade practices.

Korean policy-makers put heavy emphasis on R&D investment and technology upgrading. ... Machinery, electrical products, plastics, transportation and other chemical areas were the industries targeted to rapidly increase their R&D expenditure ratio. In addition, the National Project for R&D was established in 1982 to support public as well as public-private joint R&D projects in the high-technology fields of electronics, fine chemistry, and engineering.

The composition of export subsidies also changed dramatically. The amount of export financing for facility upgrading increased substantially during the 1980s, while financing for operational purposes decreased severely during the same period.

Table 1-6. Goals of the Five-Year Economic Development Plans: 5th through 7th

	Goals	Strategic Objectives [2]
Fifth (1982-1986)	Stabilization, Efficiency, Balance	Stabilization of the Economy Continuation of Economic Growth & Employment Balance of Regional Development & Income Equity
Sixth (1987-1991)	Advancement, Efficiency, Equity	Advancement of Economic & Social Systems Restructuring of Industries toward Technology-driven Development Regional Development & High Quality of Life

| Revised 7th [1] (1993-1997) | Building New Economy based on Citizen-Participation and Creativity | Reform of Public Finance, Banking, Taxing, and Regulation Enhancement of Growth Potential Competitiveness in the Global Market Quality of Life |

Source: Kang. 2000: 44; and the National Archives of Korea.
Note: 1) The original 7th plan (1992-1996) was replaced with the revised one (1993-1997) by the President Kim Young-sam (Presidency: 1993-1997).
2) The strategic objectives listed in the table are the selection of the main ones.

4) Performance

Despite internal and external hardships, the suffering did not last for long. South Korea, after suffering negative growth in 1980, bounced back in a few years, and continued to grow (see Table 1-7) until the country underwent the Asian Financial crisis in 1997.

Box 10 : Economic Performance in the 1980s
(Savada and Shaw, 1992: 59, 146)

In December 1983, Seoul unveiled its revised Fifth Five-Year Economic and Social Development Plan. The plan called for steady growth for the next three years, low inflation, and sharply reduced foreign borrowing. Exports were to rise by 15 percent a year, inflation was projected to be held at 1.8 percent, and per capita GNP was to rise to US$2,325 by 1986. The annual growth rate was planned to average 7.5 percent though the actual performance was higher. The real GNP growth rate was 7 percent in 1985, but for the next three years 12.9 percent, 12.8 percent, and 12.2 percent, respectively.

During the 1980s, the largest areas of government expenditure were economic services (including infrastructural projects and research and development), national defense, and education. Economic expenditures averaged several percentage points higher than defense expenditures, which remained stable at about 22 to 23 percent of the budget (about 6 percent of GNP) during the decade. In 1990 the government was studying plans to lower defense expenditures to 5 percent of GNP. Some observers noted a trend toward a slight increase in the portion of the budget devoted to social spending during the 1980s. In 1987 expenditures for social services--including health, housing, and welfare--were 16.4 percent of the budget, up from 13.9 percent in 1980, and slightly higher than 1987 government outlays for education.

Table 1- 7. The Performance of the Five-Year Economic Development Plans: 5th through 7th

(Unit: Annual Average Percentage)

	GNP		Investment		Domestic savings		Consumer price		Unemployment		Export [2]		Import [2]	
	Plan [1]	Result	Plan	Result	Plan	Result	Plan	Result	Plan	Result	Plan	Result	Plan	Result
Fifth (1982-1986)	7.5	10.3	29.1	30.3	28.1	27.7	-	3.6	4.2	4.0	11.4	10.5	8.4	4.1
Sixth (1987-1991)	7.3	10	31.6	34.0	33.5	36.3	3.0	6.8	3.7	3.6	10.0	16.4	11.0	21.0
Revised 7th (1993-1997)	6.9	7.4	35.6	36.7	35.7	35.8	3.9	5.0	-	2.4	8.2	12.6	6.9	12.8

*Source: Kang, 2000: 44; the National Archives of Korea; the Bank of Korea.
**Note: 1) The figures are based on the original targets, not the ones revised during the plan.
2) The export/import figures are based on the arrival of commodities.

5. Lessons

South Korea's rapid economic growth has been a good example of government-led development. In the take-off stage, the government planned, executed, monitored, and corrected almost every economic matter. It stood at the forefront of mobilizing foreign financial resources, and concentrated available financial resources on export-driven programs and industries with other preferential treatments. The results were phenomenal, and as a result the governing goal of building a self-sustaining economy was achieved in a relatively short time period. The self-sustaining growth machine, which enabled a virtuous circle between public finance and the market economy, provided more room for the government to expand the economy, and indeed accelerated economic growth for many years to come. In the high growth stage, South Korea re-directed its high priority industry in a timely manner from light industry to heavy and chemical industries, and to the ICT industry. Although the country underwent some critical internal and external hardships, its economy bounced back and continued its high growth rate.

What made this remarkable achievement, which was often praised as a miracle, possible? The factors are numerous, such as political stability, effective governing strategies, economic policies, export-driven growth strategy, timely transition of priority industries, disciplined entrepreneurship and labor, anti-corruption programs, continual investment in education and technology, and so on. Of these, the key factor was investment in human capital. Good governing strategies and policies would have been impossible without efficient bureaucracy. Excellent outcomes in an export-driven economy would not have been achieved without disciplined firms and the sacrifice of laborers and farmers. Furthermore, the government programs for technology & science and the family values for better education enabled continual advancement of human capital, and a timely and effective transition to the higher technology industries.

How good is the South Korean model of development for developing countries? A simple replication of Korea's development model may not guarantee the same success for other developing countries. The leadership should take into account its own country's internal and external conditions, formulate the right governing strategies, implement them with consistency, show the general public the positive results, and prepare for the next stage. But the leadership should keep in mind that the Korean model of development is not just an economic growth model, but a model of human capacity growth.

Note: This work was supported by the National Research Foundation of Korea Grant funded by the Korean Government (NRF-2013S1A3A2055108).

References

Adelman, Irma. (1999). Lessons from (S) Korea. Zagreb International Review of Economics & Business. Vol. 2, No. 2: 57-71.

Bank of Korea. (n.d.). Economic Statistics Yearbook. 1953-2012. Retrieved from http://ecos.bok.or.kr/

Bank of Korea. (n.d.). Economic Indicators [Data file]. Retrieved from http://ecos.bok.or.kr (Economic Statistics System website).

Economic Planning Board. (1982). Economic Policy in the Development Era – The 20 Year History (in Korean: 개발연대의 경제정책-경제기획원 20년사). Seoul: Economic Planning Board.

Encyclopaedia Britannica. (n.d.). Park Chung-hee. Retrieved December 10, 2013, from http://www.britannica.com/EBchecked/topic/444035/Park-Chung-Hee

Heo, Yoon. (2001). Development strategy in Korea reexamined: an interventionist perspective. The Social Science Journal. 38: 217-231.

Jaikyunghoi-Yewoohoi (in Korean: 재경회-예우회). (Eds.). (2011). Korea's Public Finance 60 Years. Seoul: Maeil Business Newspaper.

Kang, Kwang-Ha. (2000). Five-Year Economic Development Plan. Seoul: Seoul National University Press.

Mechau, Vaughn. (1961). Economic Assistance to Korea and AID Accomplishments, 1954 – 1960. Combined Economic Board.

Ministry of Finance, and Korea Development Bank. (1993). Foreign Capital and the Korean Economic Development (in Korean: 한국외자도입 30년사). Gwacheon: Ministry of Finance.

Ministry of Strategy and Finance (n.d.). The. Summary of Financial Implementation, 1950-1980. Retrieved from https://www.digitalbrain.go.kr/kor/view/library/lib02_09.jsp?code=DB0202

National Archives of Korea. (n.d.). The Economic Plan (in Korean: 경제계획). Retrieved November 19, 2013 from http://contents.archives.go.kr

National Archives of Korea. (n.d.). Presidential Election Results (in Korean: 대통령선거). Retrieved December 10, 2013, from http://theme.archives.go.kr/next/vote/outline/lineOut02.do

Savana, Andrea Matles and William Shaw (eds.). (1992). South Korea: A Country Study. Washington, D. C.: Federal Research Division, Library of Congress.

Statistics Korea. (n.d.). Economic Indicators (in Korean: 주요 경제지표) [Data file]. Retrieved from http://kosis.kr/statisticsList/statisticsList_01List.jsp?vwcd=MT_ZTITLE&parmTabId=M_01_01

World Bank. (n.d.). World Development Indicators [Data file]. Retrieved from http://data.worldbank.org

Chapter 2

E-Government of Korea:
Institutions, Policies and Laws

Cheol H. Oh (Soongsil University)

E-Government of Korea: Institutions, Policies and Laws

Cheol H. Oh (Soongsil University)

1. A General Context for e-Government in Korea

Information and communication technology (ICT) becomes a determinant factor for economic growth and social development in contemporary society. Ubiquitous computing, cloud computing, smart phone, and various kinds of social network services enable people and businesses to overcome and minimize the constraints of time and space. As industries and services rapidly cut across different traditional sectors and geographical boundaries, existing policies and rules which were defined for an analogue, single-media, and national environments are subject to change (Song & Oh, 2011).

Likewise, rapid changes, mostly caused by ICT, have played a critical role in initiating the fundamental transformation of modern governments. In general, governments are expected to do their work with limited resources; thus, policy makers are interested in maximizing the limited resources in order to attain policy goals or, simply put, to resolve social problems. In a sense, most efforts to reform governmental processes or structures can be understood as ways of improving so called administrative efficiency or effectiveness.

Traditionally, governmental reform has been often approached by functional or structural methods; e.g., rearranging existing functions among departments or creating new departments. However, the problem of such methods is they may not be useful approaches in a fundamentally different environment: i.e., the digital era. Under the circumstances, it was the potential power of ICT that naturally filled the vacuum of ideas for reform, which led to the birth of a new form of government, electronic government.

Simply put, e-Government can be understood as the utilization of the Internet and other information communication technologies in order to deliver government services to citizens online (UN &ASPA, 2002). Leading e-Government strategies in the early stage of implementation in the 80s or 90s (e.g., 'Modernizing Government' in the United Kingdom, 'e-Europe' by European Commission, Electronic Government in Korea to name a few) without exception emphasized reforming conventional or routine ways of doing business in government. As such, e-Government quickly became a global phenomenon and was swiftly adopted as an imperative to improve government services as well as internal efficiency.

Nowadays, it is easy to feel the presence of e-Government around the world, but the degree and the maturity of implementing e-Government vary depending on countries. Although the gap between developing and advanced countries in terms of e-Government tends to be narrowing, there is still a lot of work to do to close the gap. Furthermore, the recent smart revolution (e.g., SNS or smart devices) further requires and also enables governments to provide more personalized and responsive services the public.

This revolution is often called as mobile government, which utilizes mobile wireless communication technologies to deliver government services to citizens (Jaeger 2003; Ostberg 2003). This change of focus in e-Government can, no doubt, impose another burden on the shoulders of developing countries that are already behind leading e-Government countries.

Mostly, developing countries need to come up with a set of well-designed e-Government related policies and to carry out them under a strong leadership. This is where effective strategies become important. A good way of developing ideas for appropriate and effective strategies is to learn from the best practices of other leading countries. Korea has been one of such a few countries, recently proving its excellence once again by topping the 2012 UN e-Readiness evaluation.

Historically, the development of Korea's e-Government has undergone several phases. The first phase, started in the mid-1980s, was the "Pioneer Days for Foundation of e-Government ('87-'00)". At this stage, the Korean government built databases for key administrative information such as resident registration, real estate, and vehicles under the National Basic Information Systems Project, constructed the e-Government communication infrastructure through the Korea Information Infrastructure (KII) Project ('94-'97), and established an integrated infrastructure among government agencies by focusing on some tasks in limited areas (MOGAHA, 2007: 8). As a result, citizens can have access to convenient government services thanks to such DBs including issuance of certificates by making a single trip to any local office. The numbers of documents submitted to government offices are greatly reduced, and the processing time is also shortened drastically (for more detail, see NCA, 2002: 8-10).

The second phase was the "Full-Fledged Implementation of e-Government ('01-'02)". During this time period, the Korean government took a more definite shape through various national level initiatives. In particular, the Korean government implemented 11 Key Initiatives (or tasks), including the Single Window for Online Citizens Service (Government for Citizen: G4C), e-Procurement Service (G2B), and National Finance Information System (NAFIS), and set up institutional arrangements such as the legislation of the e-Government Act (March 2001). More and more government services such as patent, customs, and procurement are being provided online with improved quality of service.

The third phase was the "Advanced Development of e-Government" ('03-'07). Starting in the year 2000, policy focus was given to connecting and integrating major government business processes that had previously been dispersed and duplicated throughout government ministries and agencies. In so doing, government business was expected to be put completely into a database with the hope that citizens could more actively participate in policy making processes (NIA, 2007). Key attention was placed on the implementation of the e-Government Roadmap Project as a strategic vehicle for government innovation, thus, resulting in becoming the"World's Best Open e-Government. 31 Roadmap Projects in 4 Key Areas (Innovating Civil Services, Innovating the Way Government Works, Innovating Information Resource Management, and Reforming the Legal System) were selected. At the same time, the 'Consolidated Administrative Information Sharing System', the realization of an 'Online Participatory Democracy', and the consolidation and connection among public institutions both vertically and horizontally were also driven.

The strategic and gradual progress of e-Government initiatives enabled the Korean government to establish the technical and institutional foundation for implementing e-Government, in addition to establishing the infrastructure for sustainable government innovation, and improving services for citizens and businesses.

As Korean society is increasingly becoming ubiquitous in nature, and, thus, creating new administrative demands, the government of Korea is faced with the need to establish a new direction and role for e-Government in the context of the future administrative environment (see MOGAHA, 2007: 8-9). To meet these demands, a new strategy for e-Government, the "Master Plan for the Next Generation e-Government (2008 ~ 2012)", was prepared. As part of the Master Plan, a vision was set to build the "World's Best Digital Government inside the People." Further, a goal to offer responsive, efficient and customer-friendly services to the public was made. The vision consists of five strategies and four specific tasks that are expected to realize four goals: customer-centric customized citizen services, system-based government innovation, preventative systems for a safer society, and sustainable advancement of e-Government.

Consequently, Korea's e-Government has produced visible results: the efficiency and transparency of administrative work has been significantly improved; administrative civil services have been greatly enhanced; and opportunities for people to participate in the policy-making process have been expanded. As a result, Korea ranked first among all UN member countries in both the 2010 and 2012 UN Global E-Government Surveys in the categories of the e-Government Development Index and the e-Participation Index. Accordingly, the effectiveness of Korea's e-Government is widely acknowledged by the international community, and various e-Government systems are being exported to foreign countries.

Recently, Korea is in the process of implementing 'Smart Government', through which public users may enjoy easier and freer access to government services regardless of the delivery channel thanks to wireless information technology and converged government services (MOPAS, 2012: 4).

As illustrated above, Korea has gone through several phases or stages for a long time to build e-Government as it is, letting it continuously evolve to meet the changing demands both outside and inside the government. Under the circumstances, this study intends to share some of Korea's valuable experiences with other countries (especially developing ones), expecting them to prepare for more acceptable and relevant strategies. More importantly, such knowledge sharing is expected to prevent developing countries from otherwise making mistakes in moving back and forth while implementing e-Government policies and programs.

Along the way, many factors have been involved in steering and implementing e-Government. Among them this study is interested in examining such issues as policy systems for implementing e-Government, major policies or programs of e-Government and some of the key legal systems. In general, these issues can be understood as part of institutional building for e-Government.

Institution building is an intervention in social structures which have been established in repeated interactions between actors over a long period of time. The creation of new institutions means the change, and perhaps termination of existing institutions. Institution building must be, therefore, carried out carefully by avoiding an impulsive push or an improvised design. There must be valid grounds for building new institutions, in tackling problems which are impending, or in creating or exploiting potential opportunities in the future (Song & Oh, 2011: 18).

In the following, policy systems (or arrangements of several organizations) for implementing e-Government are first addressed in terms of coordination and planning/management. Then, some distinctive aspects of major e-Government related policies or programs are presented. Finally, one important feature of e-Government institutionalization, legal systems, is briefly examined. In addition, some implications of this study and a set of suggestions for developing countries are made.

2. Policy systems for e-Government in Korea

Policy is a set of purposive actions carried out by policy makers in dealing with social problems concerned (or perceived) by a specific target group or the public at large (Anderson, 1984). Like other public policies or programs, those for e-Government consist of life-cycle activities, e.g. plan–do–see (PDS) stage. In general, policies or programs are not completed by a single activity; rather they go through interrelated stages of policy formulation - implementation - evaluation.

Along the process, a variety of factors may influence either the dynamics of the process or the result of each stage of the process. Likewise, e-Government policy is influenced by a variety of factors such as ideas and vision of policy makers, historical and geographical conditions, social and economic composition, technological advancements, governmental institutions, and perceptions and behaviors of bureaucrats and the public.

On the other hand, any policy cannot be formulated or implemented by itself. It needs intentional pushes, and one critical push is institutions for getting the wheels of e-Government rolling. In general, policy systems for e-Government are made up of a set of institutions with different functions: e.g., coordination, formulation and/or implementation and management.

No matter how they are named, ICT-related organizations at the highest level are expected to develop a vision and strategy, draw up a set of projects and find ways to secure stable and sufficient financial resources. They suggest how ICT can innovate on society and government, facilitate national informatization, and also set specific targets for each period of a certain time duration for national development or government innovation. Then, specific organizations (e.g., OMB in the US, the MIC in Japan and the MOPAS in Korea) turn the vision into a concrete government-level ICT or e-Government plan (they may be required to send this plan to the highest agency, which later re-examines and confirms it). Each government agency develops its own ICT projects (or action plans) that contains what it should do to realize them.

1) Policy Coordination and Planning

(1) Coordination

Electronic government policy is linked to various issues including research and development, industries and e-society across different traditional sectors and geographical boundaries. As digital convergence transforms the localized dimension within an organizational unit into the whole-government dimension, institutional changes to deal with e-Government agenda are unavoidable.

With respect to policy coordination for e-Government, Korea has heavily relied on the so-called advisory committee, which also plays significant role in preparing the ground for many decisions of the top policy makers in many countries. In Korea, civil servants are recruited through competitive and merit-based general examinations and are usually rotated periodically from one job to another within a ministry or between ministries, inhibiting the accumulation of knowledge and experience in specialized policy areas. The participation of outside specialists and stakeholders in committees is, thus, strongly recommended.

In order for this advisory committee to work, liaison officers have to act as a linking pin to facilitate communication between committee members and policy makers. In Korea, the Chief of Staff to the President or the Senior Secretary for Policy & Planning usually undertakes the liaison officer role (for more detail, see Song & Oh, 2011: 25-30).

In the first stage (1987-1995), the National Basic Information System project was managed by the Information Network Supervisory Commission (INSC) chaired by the Chief of Staff to the President. The Chief of Staff to the President managed the overall aspects of the project as the Commissioner of the Commission. He played a leading role in resolving inter-ministerial conflicts, and supervised necessary measures for standardization and security, the sharing of ICT resources, as well as obtaining financial resources. This stage was typically driven by the President's strong will to mobilization and leadership.

The second stage saw the launching of the Informatization Promotion Committee (IPC) chaired by the Prime Minister, in which the Ministry of Information and Communication (MIC) played a major role as a lead ministry in implementing the High-speed Broadband Network Plan and Informatization Promotion Framework Plan (IPFP). Overall, the MIC effectively drove the IPFP agenda by mobilizing the Informatization Promotion Fund (IPF) and technical and manpower resources of the National Computerization Agency (later changed to National Information Society Agency).

In parallel to these institutional arrangements, the Presidential e-Government Special Committee (PEGSP) (2001-2007) was formed and dealt with the president's e-Government agendas. This committee, linked with government reform, was typically a governance structure in which many outside technical experts outside participated in managing multi-ministry or government-wide projects, under the strong support of the President.

The MIC, the Ministry of Government Administration & Home Affairs (MOGAHA), and the Ministry of Planning and Budget (MPB) participated together in PEGSP as a collaboration body. The Senior Secretary to the President for Policy & Planning, as a counterpart of the civilian chairman, engaged in the overall process of implementing the President's projects.

In the third stage, the President's Council on National ICT Strategies (PCIS) was created, replacing PEGSP, on the basis of the enactment of National Informatization Framework (NIFP) and co-chaired by both the Prime Minister and a civilian expert. In the institutional settings of NIFP and PCIS, the Ministry of Public Administration and Security (MOPAS), replacing the Ministry of Information and Communication (MIC), takes over the role of the lead agency in implementing ICTD policy in general. It, however, takes time to realize the performance of new institutional arrangements (for more detail, see the table in Song & Oh, 2011: 36-37).

Figure 2-1. Current Organizational Structure for ICT of Korea

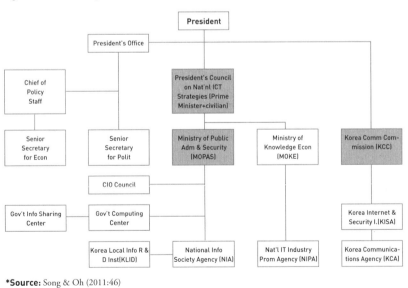

*Source: Song & Oh (2011:46)

(2) Planning and Management

One feasible strategy for improved planning and management across various departments of government is to create a ministry in full charge of ICTD policy within which numerous closely related functions or programs are all included. In Korea, an integrated ICT ministry replaced the Ministry of Post & Telecommunication (MPT), which was privatized or devolved into executive agencies or public enterprises since the 1980s. ICT policy agendas including e-Government came to fill in the policy vacuum arising from privatization or devolution of postal and telecommunication services of the MPT. If the ICT ministry had a limited leadership in technical expertise and financial resources, ICT policy agendas would have remained outside the socio-economic development realm as well as broad public sector reform including e-Government.

Despite the creation of an integrated ministry, conflicts occurred mainly between the MIC and other Ministries like MOGAHA (later changed to MOPAS) and MOCIE (later changed to MOKE) surrounding e-Government and ICT industry. For example, a sharp conflict between the MIC and MOGAHA around the jurisdiction for a government computing center had lasted for years until the direct intervention of the President.

In 2008, the integrated functions of the MIC (1995-2007) were broken into several ministries: KCC, MOPAS and MOKE. There were two main reasons for the reorganization of ICTD policy. One was to consolidate the main functions of the MIC and Korea Broadcasting Commission (KBC) into the Korea Communication Commission (KCC) in aggressive preparation for digital convergence. The other was to mitigate the conflicts between the MIC and other ministries dealing with some sub-functions of ICTD policy. Likewise, public bodies under the umbrella of the former

MIC such as NIA, NIPA, KISA, and KCA were each disassembled into MOPAS, MCST, MOKE, and KCC.

(3) CIO

According to the National Informatization Framework Act of 2009, CIOs in ministries and agencies have the responsibilities of coordination, support and evaluation of informatization programs, linkage between informatization policy and other policies, management of information resources, promotion of digital culture and bridging the digital divide, development of enterprise architecture, and education and training of human resources for ICT policies including e-Government.

The Assistant Minister for Planning and Management (AMPM) in ministries and agencies assumes the position of the ministry CIO by the support of directors with technical expertise. The AMPM assumes the overall tasks of the ministry including planning and budget, legal affairs, monitoring and evaluation, congressional matters, and miscellaneous tasks not affiliated with other offices and bureaus in the ministry. ICT policy agenda is, however, hard to be prioritized by the AMPM. Moreover, the AMPM does not have sufficient substantive and technical expertise in the ICT policy area. That is why they need to be aided by experts inside departments.

Korea's CIOC chaired by the Minister of MOPAS is composed of AMPMs of 25 ministries and agencies. It deals with formulation and implementation of e-Government related policies, administrative information sharing, establishment of enterprise architecture, and standardization of ICT. CIOC, however, does not function as well as expected due to lower priorities and technical expertise in ICTD policy and programs.

Table 2-1. CIOs and CIO Council in Korea

	CIO	CIO Council
Member	Assistant Minister for Planning & Management of ministries and agencies	Chairman: MOPAS Minister Member: CIOs of ministries
Mission	1. Comprehensive coordination, support & evaluation of informatization programs 2. Linkage between informatization & other policy areas 3. Support of administrative work through ICT 4. Management of information resources 5. Promotion of digital culture and bridging digital divide 5. Development of enterprise architecture 7. Education & training of ICTD manpower	1. Formulation and implementation of e-Government related policies 2.Administrative information sharing 3. Enterprise architecture 4. Systematic management and standardization of ICT resources 5. Multi-agency and government-wide e-Government related projects

*Source: The National Informatization Framework Law of Korea, §11, §12.

Historically, in Korea, the Chief of Staff to the President or Senior Secretary for Policy and Planning played a crucial role in planning and implementing major projects since the 1980s. He was strongly empowered by the President in terms of mobilization of financial, manpower, and technical resources. This fact may become an obstacle to the activities of CIOC. It is also more convenient for technical staff in computing units of ministries to directly rely upon the supra-ministry organization such as presidential committees or other empowered organizations rather than CIOC managed by the MOPAS. Because ICT policy has often been managed as the President's agenda, the CIOC system chaired by the Minister of Public Administration and Security does not work well in resolving the competing interests between ministries and drawing cooperation. Competing ministries tend to hesitate to cooperate with the MOPAS because they are likely to cast doubt on policy neutrality carried out by the MOPAS.

2) Implementation and Post-Management

(1) Organizations for Implementing e-Government

No matter how ICT policy or e-Government is defined, it needs innovative ideas and a set of decisions, strategies and plans to mobilize organizations and resources for successful implementation. It is simply because policy implementation is not an automatic process following policy formation. Rather, it needs a push to make it move in the way it is designed. More specifically, a variety of organizations are often involved in the whole process of making and managing e-Government projects. As one of critical factors for the successful implementation of policies is organization (Jones, 1984), institutional systems for securing resources and effective execution in the policy process have been regarded as crucial.

Since it is hard for government agencies to adapt swiftly to the rapidly changing ICT environment and to come up with effective strategies on their own, they tend to rely on research institutes or other organizations that can provide technical or policy support. Likewise, as a social and technical system, e-Government requires appropriate information technology or policy support to carry out what is expected from it (e.g., enhancing administrative efficiency or proper delivery of government services to the target population etc).

To this end, the Korean government has utilized government affiliated research institutes such as the Korea Information Society Development Institute (KISDI), the Korea Information Security Agency (KISA), and the Electronics and Telecommunications Research Institute (ETRI). They have served as part of key think-tanks in national informatization (including e-Government) by directly or indirectly engaging in various activities like planning, implementing and evaluating informatization projects.

Under the circumstances, it is interesting to examine organizations taking up important tasks in the process of implementation, more specifically, who those support organizations are and how they can help the government implement ICT-related policies or programs (for more detail on support agencies, see Bhatnagar, 2001).

One of the critical support agencies for implementing e-Government in Korea is the National Information Society Agency (NIA). It was founded as the National Computerization Agency in 1987, authorized to provide technical consulting services for e-Government in 2001, designated as the chief managing body of Korea's e-Government Project in 2004, and in 2009 it became a new agency by merging KADO (Korea Agency for Digital Opportunity & Promotion) of which the main function was to eliminate the digital divide and build a healthy information culture.

As it is related to implementing e-Government, the following highlights some of its major roles:

- Execute a knowledge-based electronic government project that emphasizes communication, cooperation, and trust.
  - Execute integration and linking of projects to improve the communications and benefit of the people, and active economic activities.
  - Build a sustainable base for informatization, protect information safely, and reinforce information security.
- Support the planning of IT-related policy and specialized technology.
  - Support the informatization policy, including the establishment of the direction for advanced strategic informatization projects.
  - Support outstanding informatization issues for each department and area of the government, including a national informatization

execution plan review.

- Promote "Low Carbon Green Informatization" by utilizing information technology.
    - Support the establishment of a policy for "green informatization,"
      and the execution plan of each department.
    - Develop and support standards for stimulating green ICT, and or-
      ganize and operate green ICT associations (Song & Oh, 2011: 80-81).

(2) Post-implementation Management and Evaluation

The execution of government policy does not automatically result in expected effects by simply delivering services to target groups or imposing
regulations. Appropriate management is needed to create such effects at
the right time, and a systematic analysis is required if the expected effects
seem to be insufficient.

The core purpose of evaluation activities is to realize an efficient evaluation through systematic controlling and management of the whole process
of evaluation. Accordingly, there are some issues to be examined at each
stage of the evaluation process, and management should be performed to
create linkages among them. First, as shown in Figure 2-2., the evaluation
environment forms the requirement (condition) for systematic analysis according to the progress of specific programs designed by e-Government
programs. Once an e-Government program progresses, the evaluation
input factors (e.g., manpower, organization, equipment, budget, etc.) are provided
and the evaluation is done according to the schedule. The process, then,
leads to the result, which is the evaluation outcome. Evaluation outcomes
work as a piece of information on the feedback loops that may be considered in not only program evaluation, but in designing new e-Government

Figure 2-2. Management Model of e-Government Program Evaluation

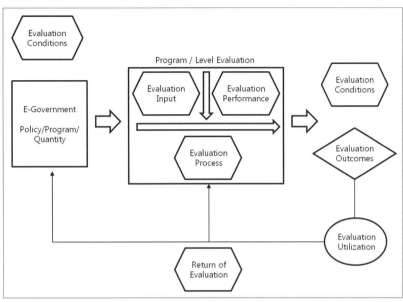

*Source: Oh (2012:4)

policies and programs (for more detail on ICT program evaluation in Korea, see Oh & Myeong, 2002).

The core point of discussing post-implementation management is about what, when and how to manage programs which are already implemented. That is, programs will operate more effectively if these terms are prescribed beforehand as part of program or policy procedure. There are a few conceptual points to consider if the post-implementation management is to be performed.

First, the responsibility for the overall management of e-Government programs needs to rest with the department in charge. The plans for post-management will be considered to a certain extent beforehand in the department that drafts and executes e-Government programs. The specific execution of such a plan may be done cooperatively with other departments within the institute, or other outside organizations. Depending on the circumstances of individual countries, a leading agency (e.g., a higher independent organization like president's committees) may, however, manage the whole process of evaluation. Individual departments may, thus, have little direct role in evaluation but provide required evaluation-related data to the agency).

Another issue that policy makers need to consider for the successful evaluation is the education about informatization. One of the problems faced at the initial stage of informatization is the insufficient recognition of an informatization among the members of government. Expanding and raising an informatization mind-set is a critical factor that affects the success of informatization like e-Government. Accordingly, adequate contents and methods for informatization education need to be developed and managed within the organization while an informatization program is being executed.

Finally, policy makers need to consider the environmental changes that may occur. That is, the chances that problems caused by a specific e-Government program occur need to be lowered by systematically monitoring the effect of the program and/or by making modifications if required.

3. Major Policies (Programs) for e-Government

The shape of e-Government is to a great extent reflected in related policies and programs. Perhaps, the major responsibility, if any, of any organizations in charge of e-Government is to come up with a set of well-mapped policies or programs, targeting specific problems and, thus, creating new values or attaining desirable goals. Likewise, e-Government policies or programs are suggested and implemented to resolve problems facing governments.

For example, enhancing administrative efficiency and improving service delivery are often cited as the reasons for employing ICT to innovate governmental processes, that is, building e-Government.

However, e-Government cannot be built overnight. It requires a series of well-designed and coordinated activities over a certain period of time. Further, the vision, strategies or policies of e-Government are likely to change or evolve along the way, depending on the policy environment, changes in needs or perspectives of regimes (leadership) to name a few.

Korea is not an exception. It has gone through several stages of developing e-Government over the past two decades. In so doing, several administrations have come and gone, implementing major watershed policies and witnessing rapid development of e-Government as a result of consistent efforts at government innovation.

Looking back on the history of e-Government implementation in Korea, it is easy to find that the weight and value of e-Government implementation have changed from enhancing the efficiency of public administration through the computerization of government works until the 1990s to increasing satisfaction and active participation of citizens in policy-making since the 2000s. Today, e-Government is considered the government's key management system that serves as an infrastructure for developing and improving the foundation for a democratic society and national competitiveness.

Although many different policies and programs have been developed and implemented to build e-Government in Korea, the so-called 11 initiatives (or killer projects) of the Kim Administration starting in 2001 and 31 initiatives during the Rho Administration made a significant impact. In addition, the current Lee Administration's major projects are in the middle of completion with a target to fundamentally reform the face of government.

In the following section, some characteristic features of two administrations (i.e., the Rho, Mu-hyun and the current Lee, Myung-bak Administration) which are worth noting will be briefly examined.

1) e-Government in the Rho Administration (2003-2007)

(1) Vision and Objectives

The Rho Administration's vision of e-Government was to build the world's best open e-Government. The following highlights the core of what was to be achieved during the Rho Mu-hyun Administration (see PCID, 2003: 6-10).

Figure 2-3. The Rho Administration's vision of e-Government

The Rho Administration intended to achieve three major policy goals, and each goal was given specific levels of performance as follows

- Civil Services Goals: drastically enhancing efficiency in administrative processes in civil and business services without visiting the relevant offices and raising the rank of business support competitiveness to 10th place.

Table 2-2. Goals of Improving Civil Services

Item	2003	2008
Online Work Processes	15%	85%
Business Support Competitiveness	24th	10th
Number of visits to District Offices	10/year	Under 3/year
e-Government Usage Rate	23%	60%

- Administrative Efficiency Goals: Expanding the electronization of work processes and sharing of documents; enhancing efficiency through integrated management of information resources enabling real time administration.

Table 2-3. Goals of Improving Administrative Efficiency

Item	2003	2008
Cross Agency Work Processes	Partial electronization, not yet integrated Personnel, finance, inspection etc.	Overall electronization, integration
Electronization of Documents	Coexistence of paper and e-documents	Unify into e-documents
Sharing of Information	Limited cross agency sharing	Complete cross agency sharing
Management of Information Resources	Diffused, independent	Unified, integrated

- Administrative Democracy Goals: Enhancing political participation by providing administrative information and strengthening citizens' power of controlling personal information.

Table 2-4. Goals of Improving Administrative Democracy

Item	2003	2008
Electronic Participation	Public opinion polls	Policy participation and consultation
Openness of Administrative Info	Passive and limited	Active and open
Privacy Protection	Risk of Privacy Invasion	Reinforce control over personal information

(2) **Key Agendas and Roadmaps** (Implementing Plans)

As policies are not automatically implemented, well-mapped plans are needed before putting several policies or programs into effect. In this regard, the Rho Administration prepared a set of agendas and specific time tables (or roadmaps) of programs for carrying out the agendas.

The Rho Administration initiated 31 so-called major projects, which can be understood as a mix of former e-Government programs and newly added ones. The initiatives consisted of 4 sectors, 10 agendas, 31 major projects, and 45 unit projects. It's roadmap included firstly, integrating and expanding the infrastructure from a multi-department network to a nation-wide network; secondly, developing interactive websites (Q&A, FAQ, etc.), and details for enhancing participation by customers, civic groups, and the general population in government policy activities to ensure transparency in civil services; and thirdly, advancing the integration of the government's functions, information resources, and other core activities throughout the government (President's Committee of Government Innovation & Decentralization, 2005: 50-52).

Table 2-5. Policy Areas and Agendas in the Rho Administration

Policy Areas	Agendas
Government Internal Process Reform (G2G)	1. Establishing electronic procedures 2. Expanding common use of public info. 3. Service oriented BPR
Public Service Reform (G2C, G2B)	4. Enhancement of the civil service 5. Enhancement of business service 6. Expanding electronic civil participation
Information Resource Management Reform (Common Platform)	7. Integration/standardization of info. Resource 8. Strengthening of information protection system 9. Specialization of the IT manpower and organization
Legal System Reform	10. Consolidation of e-Government related legal system

*Source: PCID (2007:17)

- As an example of roadmaps, the following shows the case of 'Establishing Electronic Procedures.'

Table 2-6. Roadmaps for Establishing Electronic Procedures

Main Activities	Phase 1			Phase 2	
Year	'03	'04	'05	'06	07
Paperless Administration	Electronic document creation and storage				
	Basic plan	DB of main national ledgers			
	Reforming legal system	Centralization of electronic ledger			
Informatization of common government-wide processes	Advancement of common administration system (Finance, Budgeting, HR)				
	Identify new tasks for common process	Informatization of new task (Audit, Publicity, International Relation)			
Local e-Government	Local financial System ISP	Standard System Development	Implementation of the financial system to all local governments		
	Deployment of unified administration information system				
		Development and advancement of converged portal system of the central and local governments			

*Source: PCID (2003:19)

More interestingly, specific sub-programs were also managed by their own timetables for implementation over a certain period of time. The following shows the roadmap for 'Electronic Document Processing' in the category of paperless administration under establishing electronic procedures agenda.

- Expansion and enhancement of electronic document distribution system (EDDS)
  - Expansion of intermediate system to secure credibility and stability
  - Enhancement of EDDS for all central government agencies
  - Convergence of EDDS with administration information system

- Deployment of public records archiving and management system
  - Deployment after committee's review of the plan

- Electronic conversion of all document ledger and discontinuance of paper ledgers

Table 2-7. Roadmaps for Electronic Document Processing

Item	'03	'04	'05	'06	'07
Expansion and enhancement of EDDS	2nd Phase EDDS expansion	ISP for EDDS enhancement	System Deployment	Expansion of EDDS	
Deployment of public records archiving system	Plan review	Development of records archiving system		System stability and enhancement	
Electronic conversion of document ledgers	Planning	DB of main national ledgers			
	Legal reform	Electronic conversion			

*Source: PCID (2003:46)

2) e-Government in the Lee Administration (2008-2012)

(1) Vision and Goals

Over the last two decades, the focus of e-Government implementation has changed from single department infrastructure to networking of back office and front office and, then, to networking of multi-departments and, finally, total integration of nationwide government branches. This change reflects the underlying value of user-focused (or -centered) service delivery of e-Government (see Vergez, 2006; Oh, 2011).

Built on the progress of informatization promotion in individual ministries and the level of e-Government development, the Lee Myung-bak administration, inaugurated in 2008, has been pursuing quality management by maturing e-Government through a shift of focus from 'promotion' and 'construction' to 'utilization' and 'connection'. Further, the frameworks for e-Government implementation were put under the full responsibility of the Ministry of Public Administration and Security with improved legal systems (see MOGAHA, 2007: 16-35)

Figure 2-4. Vision and Goals of e-Government in the Lee Administration

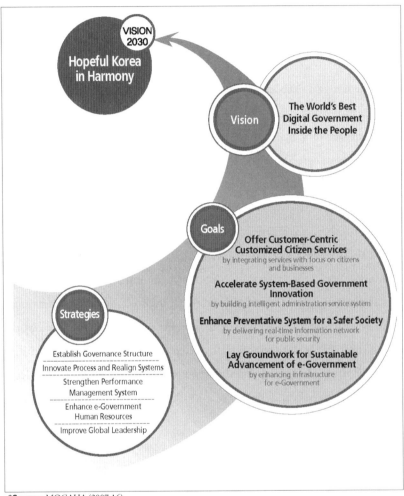

*Source:** MOGAHA (2007:16)

(2) Implementation Strategies

- Establishing Governance Structure: Establishing a system where all stakeholders including industrial players, academia, research institutes, and government can participate; strengthening partnership between central-local governments and establishing a system for compromise and mediation centered around the CIOs of each government entity; establishing processes for collecting citizens' consensus on all the procedures in digital government projects, and operating policy-client groups (users' groups for verification).

- Innovating Process and Realign Systems: Reforming the legal system and innovating work procedures that are used as preconditions for the development of inter-ministry processes; improving regulations suitable for electronic public administration and public-private partnerships.

- Strengthening Performance Management System: Establishing performance management processes such as setting measurement criteria and goals, regular performance measuring, and evaluation-feedback, introducing a contract system based on performance evaluation between supervising and commissioned agencies, and investment on the basis of 'selection and concentration' methods; establishing an e-Government service quality management system such as quality management, change management, and measurement of service and operation levels.

- Enhancing e-Government Human Resources: Training IT experts specializing in such sectors as project management and security and developing careers for IT experts; providing IT-oriented training programs customized for CEO, CIO, and staff

- Improving Global Leadership: Enhancing e-Government cooperation with international organizations and foreign countries and expanding global presence; strengthening support for international standardization, international authentication and promoting the Korean Model of e-Government

(3) Key Agendas and Tasks

The 24 key initiatives of the Master Plan for Next Generation e-Government were selected from 396 candidate tasks, based on research for selecting future e-Government initiatives, survey results from all government agencies, analysis of the 50 key initiatives of VISION 2030, and identification of new e-Government initiatives.

Table 2-8. Goals, Agendas and 24 Key Initiatives

Goals/agendas	24 Key Initiatives
Service Integration based on the Needs of Citizens and Businesses(10) ① Integration of Services Delivery System enabling easier public access ② Integration of Business Information Services for enhanced corporate Competitiveness	Integrated citizen support services Customized e-Government services (My e-Gov) Integrated services for culture and tourist information Comprehensive education information services Comprehensive user-oriented legislative information services Integrated open national border management services Integrated administrative support services for businesses Comprehensive national defense industry management service Globally integrated e-logistics network Comprehensive land information management system
Intelligent Government Work Systems (5) ③ Digital government Network for Facilitatingmultiagency collaboration ④ Transparent Policy Decision Making Systems and enhanced sharing of administrative information	Digital national governance system Advanced local e-Government and integrated local IT network GIS-based administrative support system Shared services for customized administrative information E-court services
Real-time Public Safety Information Network (6) ⑤ Enhanced National Defence and Safety Management Systems ⑥ Intelligent Public Order Management System	Share services for foreign affairs and trade information Digital national emergency response system Real-time disaster prevention management system Intelligent environment monitoring system Comprehensive customer safety information services Public order management information services

Strengthened e-Government Basic Infrastructure (3) ⑦ Stronger Information Security and Privacy Protection for enhanced public trust in e-Government ⑧ Universal e-Government Services ⑨ Enhanced Sharing of Information Resources for stronger e-Government infrastructure	Integrated e-Government service authentication system Universal e-Government services and usage promotion Infrastructure for e-Government shared services

*Source: NIA (2010); MOGAHA (2007:19)

These 24 key initiatives support the integrated infrastructure for sharing administrative information among government agencies and share the common goal of stimulating continual innovation in the public sector. Thus, the promotion of innovation was one of the main selection criteria. At the same time, weight was placed on candidate initiatives that were high on the agenda in terms of need for informatization and impact outcome, but those that were not able to be implemented due to barriers to initiation.

Through the 24 Key Initiatives selected to achieve the Four Goals of the Next Generation e-Government, the Korean government is trying to further advance the current e-Government level for smarter, faster, and better service delivery.

4. A Brief Look at Legal Frameworks

The success of building e-Government depends on the timely establishment of a proper legal framework. Existing rules and regulations were defined for an analogue and mono-media environment, inhibiting cross-cutting services beyond different traditional sectors and geographical boundaries. Laws aim primarily at providing predictability, fostering order-ly and efficient operations of ministries, providing a basis for administrative accountability, reducing the scope for arbitrary behavior, and defending the ministries when its regulatory decisions are challenged. Without timely and proper legislations, those aims are hardly achievable. Institutions for e-Government policies or programs should encourage and facilitate the formulation of new legislations for sound e-Governance.

There are two approaches to ICT related legislations. One is to enact an all-encompassing basic or framework law to deal with the promotion and regulations together. This approach is found in the cases of Japan's ICT Basic Law and Korea's National Informatization Framework Law. They stipulate comprehensively the core elements of administrative statutes including the establishment of relevant agencies and their responsibilities. The promotion and regulation of ministries derives from these legislative statutes.

Another approach is to enact individual laws regarding ICT policies and/or programs according to specific needs for legislation. In this regard, there are two types of ICT laws: promotion (e.g., e-Government, government innovation and performance management, industrial promotion) and regulations (e.g., privacy, information security, harmful and unlawful contents).

In the following, a brief summary of both framework for national infor-matization and an individual law for e-Government in Korea is presented (for more detail, see Song & Oh, 2011: 56-57).

1) Framework Law

The Korean government has long relied upon the framework act system since its initiation of ICT policy. The Informatization Promotion Framework Act (IPFA) was enacted in 1995 to effectively implement the informatization of the state and sectors of society, and also to strategically promote the IT industry. In 2008, the National Informatization Framework Law (NIFL), the revised version of IPFA, was enacted. The main content was to rebuild governance structure, with other stipulations remaining almost unchanged. The supra-ministerial coordinating committee for ICT changes from Informatization Promotion Committee (chairman: Prime Minister) to President's Council on National ICT Strategies (co-chairman: prime minister and a civilian), and lead agency also changed from the former MIC to the Ministry of Public Administration and Security (MOPAS). Legal and regulatory frameworks of ICTD policy under the new law (NIFL) can be summarized as in Table 2-9.

Table 2-9. Legal and regulatory framework of ICT policy in Korea

Classification	Item	Law
Framework		National Informatization Framework Law
Informatization of State and Society	E-government & public informatization	E-Gov, Civil Applications, Task Process, Civil Registration, Public Records, Public Info Disclosure, Distance Court, Location Based Info, Geographical Info, Judicial Process
	Establishment of favourable environments for utilization	E-signature, E-transaction, Copyright, Internet Address Resources, Trade, Personal Info Protection, Traffic, E-Check, E-Financial Transaction, E-library, E-procurement
	Prevention of information society dysfunctions	Privacy Protection, E-credit Info, Communication Info Protection, Telecom, Critical Infrastructure, Consumer protection, Criminal
Sustainable Development of IT & industry	Establishment of basis for ICT industry and ICT based industry	Software Industry Promotion, Digital Contents Industry, Broadcasting, Internet Multimedia Business, E-Learning Industry, Game Industry Promotion, Audio Industry Promotion, Intelligent Robotics, ICT Industry Promotion
Advancement of IT infrastructure	Building and Upgrading of ICT Networks	Privacy Protection, Telecom Carriers, Frequency and Spectrum, ICT Enterprises, Broadcasting & Com Development, Construction, Road

Source: http://www.law.go.kr/

Firstly, the government is required to promote measures for forming an advanced information and telecommunications network society in light of the urgency to adapt to the world's rapid and drastic changes in the socio-economic structure caused by the utilization of ICT.

Secondly, its basic measures are: integrated promotion of the further expansion of advanced information and telecommunication networks, enrichment of contents, and learning of the skills for utilizing information; formation of the world's most advanced information and telecommunications networks, promotion of fair competition, and other measures; upgrading of people's skills for utilizing information and development of expert human resources; reformation of regulations and facilitation of e-commerce through appropriate protection and exploitation of intellectual property rights, etc.

Thirdly, the government should set forth a priority policy program expeditiously and intensively in accordance with the basic ideas and the basic measures, and published via the Internet.

2) Promotion Laws for e-Government

Few countries except Korea and the US have the laws focusing only on e-Government. The US e-Government Act of 2002 stipulates the creation of the Office of e-Government and IT in the OMB with a federal CIO appointed by the President, and the codification and expansion of commitment to customer-focused service development. It establishes an e-Government Fund, administered by the General Service Administration (GSA), to support ICT projects approved by the OMB that enable federal government to conduct activities electronically.

The Korean government enacted the Electronic Government Law in

2001. It stipulates principles like enhancing a linkage between government innovation and electronic services, improving citizens' convenience, innovating business processes, and promoting electronic management in order to improve the efficiency and productivity of public administration as well as the quality of civil service. In particular, details about administrative information sharing are stipulated in the revised Law from 2010. This chapter may be benchmarked by countries that are interested in expanding information sharing across ministries with the issues of strengthening the protection of privacy and information security.

Table 2-10. Information Sharing Stipulations of e-Government Law in Korea

§36: Duty of information sharing, and prohibition of overlapped collection

§37: Establishment of Administrative Information Sharing Center in the MOPAS

§38: Objects of shared information

§39: Applications and approval of information sharing

§40: Examination, approval and deliberation of agenda

§41: Revocation and standstill of information sharing

§42: Pre-agreement of information subject

§43: The right to request for confirmation of information subject

§44: Request for fees

*Source: http://www.law.go.kr, http://elaw.klri.re.kr/

5. Conclusion

Institutions are multi-purpose vehicles, either promoting or regulating the mutual interactions when dealing with various policy problems. Countries, whether advanced or developing, adopt several public governance models in pursuit of a variety of objectives of ICT policies including e-Government. There is no 'one best way' or 'one size fits all' solution to the question of what the best strategies for implementing e-Government are. After a variety of discussions, a core aim of such strategies is to design acceptable and relevant institutional arrangements for e-Government depending on individual countries. There are, however, some lessons which policy makers and public officials in developing countries need to keep in mind.

Institutional mechanisms must fit the policy context to which a country is constrained. There are large variations among countries in relying upon those institutions to deal with e-Government policy agendas efficiently and effectively. Not all institutional building is guaranteed to be a success; rather, it is easily subject to failure. The creation of a new institution may be easy and involves little cost in one country, but quite difficult, and invoive huge cost in another. Various conditions and factors will determine the degree of difficulty and cost of implementing e-Government.

In general, governance of ICT continues to change toward a greater centralization of ICT policy issues. It is, however, quite the reverse to the decentralization, delegation and devolution trends of administrative functions in many countries in recent decades. Centralized governance needs coordination, cooperation and collaboration among relevant actors. Collaboration continues to be encouraged, with an even stronger emphasis on collaboration across sectors to create a networked society (UNDESA, 2008:73).

It is more realistic to divide institutional arrangements for planning and coordinating ICT and e-Government policy agendas into supra-ministerial and ministerial levels. Many countries like the U.S., Japan, and Korea have been operating integrated and upgraded institutions for promoting the functions of government-wide ICT policy since the 1990s.

A common factor to those countries is strong leadership and continued commitment of presidents and prime ministers. Top policy makers have to pay attention to establishing the proper role and missions of government and ministerial CIOs and the CIO council. CIOs and the CIO council can initiate integrated ICT and e-Government policy agenda by bridging ICTs and socio developments as well as government innovation.

On the other hand, the establishment of mid- to long-term master plans (or policies or programs) based upon the framework law is crucial to the continuous and consistent implementation of national informatization or e-Government. The Korean government has successfully developed and implemented several master plans and projects including the National Database Projects, the High-Speed Networks Projects, Cyber Korea 21, and various e-Government plans. Most of them were continuously and consistently driven and completed within the deadlines despite the transition of government administrations.

Based on the experiences of developing and implementing the master plans, the following factors need to be considered as critical success factors in the process of making master plans:

- Establishment of clear vision and objectives
- Analysis of the past and present situations
- Development of strategies and action plans
- Development of roadmap and milestones
- Mobilization of financial, human and technical resources
- Institutional rearrangements with lead and relevant ministries, and public bodies
- Continuous monitoring and systematic performance management

In addition, top policy makers should consider values and interests that are systematically excluded or under-represented by existing institutions. They should not be inspired merely by the primary motives of effectiveness or efficiency, but by encompassing values like political legitimacy, social integration, and government transparency, when implementing e-Government. It is ICT or e-Government policy that pursues these values. It is, thus, important to keep exploring the needs for new strategies or policy directions that fit better with individual countries to cope with the changing policy environment.

Note: This article was funded by and reported to Korea Eximbank in 2012.

References

Anderson, James E. (1984). Public Policy-Making, third edition. New York: Holt, Rinehart and Winston.

Bhatnagar, S. (2001). *"Enabling e-Government in Developing Countries: from Vision to Implementation"*. World Bank.

Government Innovation and Decentralization Committee. (2005). *E-Government of the Participatory Government*. Seoul: Government Innovation and Decentralization Committee, Republic of Korea.

Jaeger, P. T. (2003). The endless wire: E-Government as a global phenomenon. *Government Information Quarterly*, 20(4): 323–331

Jones, C. (1984). *An Introduction to the Study of Public Policy*. Belmont, CA: Wadsworth.

Ministry of Government Administration and Home Affairs, MOGAHA. (2007). *Master Plan for the Next Generation e-Government in Korea*.

Ministry of Public Administration and Security, MOPAS (2012). *E-Government of Korea: Best Practices.*

National Computerization Agency, NCA. (2002). *E-Government in Korea.*

National Information Society Agency, NIA. (2007). *Toward a Ubiquitous Society: e-Government in Korea.*

National Information Society Agency, NIA. (2010). *Informatization White Paper.*

Oh, Cheol H. (2011). "Citizen Participation on the web: the case of 'epeople' in Korea" in Holzer, M., Kong, D. and Bromberg, A. (eds.) *Citizen Participation: Innovative and Alternative Modes for Engaging Citizens.* National Center for Public Performance, Newark, NJ: Rutgers University: 119-136.

Oh, Cheol H. (2012). "An Understanding of e-Government".*a paper presented at UNPOG.*

Oh, Cheol H. & Myeong, S.H. (2002). Evaluating e-Government. *International Review of Public Administration*, 7(2): 33-43.

Ostberg, O. (2003). "A Swedish View on Mobile Government," *2003 International Symposium on Digital Mobility and Mobile Government*, KISDI: 67-78.

President's Committee of Government Innovation & Decentralization, PCID. (2003). *E-Government Roadmap*.

Song, Hee-jun & Oh, Cheol H. (2011). *ICT for Development Institution Building*. UN-APCICT/ESCAP.

United Nations, & American Society for Public Administration (ASPA). (2002). *Benchmarking e-Government: A Global Perspective*. New York: U.N. Publications.

Vergez, Christian. (2006). "E-Government as a Tool for Change" *paper presented at Global E-Government Conference towards a More Competent and Trustful e-Government* (Seoul, Korea: 26 May).

Chapter 3

Case study on the Introduction of eProcurement

Eungkeol Kim (Public Procurement Service)

Case study on the Introduction of eProcurement

Eungkeol Kim (Public Procurement Service)

1. Policies for the introduction of eProcurement

1) Importance of domestic public procurement

Governmental procurement is divided into central procurement and de-centralized procurement according to the procurement method. Central procurement operates in a system of conducting procurement operations for public institutions, and is usually adopted from countries which emphasize effective execution of their purchase budget. On the other hand, decentralized procurement operates in a way in which public institutions implement self-regulating procurement operations, and is usually adopted by countries where decentralized entities possess power or have established their municipal systems.

The operation method of our country is a limited central procurement system which includes the combination of central procurement and decentralized procurement. In terms of governmental institutions, goods and services worth more than KRW 100 million won and constructions worth more than KRW 3 billion won are obligated to request a contract with the Public Procurement Service(PPS). However, the local government and public enterprises can arbitrarily decide upon the request of the contract in the PPS regardless of the amount.

As the market liberalization progressed and the local government system introduced in 1994 became stabilized, the central procurement system became weaker than before. However, considering how the PPS, the public procurement institution, executes more than 30% of all procurement in the public sector of our country, it is true that the central procurement system still possesses significant influence.

The contribution to the efficient execution of the budget through the minimization of government procurement costs may be the greatest foundation of central procurement. However, when considering the enormous influence which government procurement has on the national economy, they must carry on the roles of supporting small and medium-sized, female-owned, and socially discriminated businesses as well as gaining transparency and justice for the procurement administration throughout the process.

Unlike the private sector, which puts profit making as the priority, the procurement of the public sector needs to consider the influence which it may have on the national economy. Therefore, not only the efficiency but the public must also be pursued. Particularly, real economy supportive functions such as the support provided for the socially discriminated businesses cannot be expected from other institutions besides the PPS, and since public procurement possesses an important role as the government's method of market interference for real economic support, it is an important function which cannot be weakened because of the securement of effectiveness.

Table 3-1. Performance of domestic central procurement

Classification		2010	2011
Total Procurement Volume		104.4 trillion won	99.8 trillion won
Trade Volume on KONEPS	Total	75.1 trillion won	63.8 trillion won
	Central procurement	39.1 trillion won	35.0 trillion won
	Own procurement	36.0 trillion won	28.8 trillion won

2) Background of the introduction of eProcurement

Ever since the 1990s, eProcurement has become situated as one of the most important agendas in public sector reform. Particularly, since the authoritative administrative system of the era which prioritizes development came to an end and a new democratic administrative model was being searched for, the construction of an effective and just procurement administration system of the procurement market which causes great influence on the national economy has been recognized as an important reform task in the public sector. The following is the background for the cause which led eProcurement to be recognized as an important measure for the procurement administration reform.

(1) Increase in demand for transparency & fairness for public procurement

Governmental procurement differs from the private procurement which prioritizes effectiveness & economic feasibility. As it should not only seek for logical value which emphasizes the resulting point of view of the fund enforcement, but should also pursue moral value which secures legitimacy of the fund enforcement procedures such as transparency and fairness. If consideration is given that the source of funds of governmental procurement is from taxes paid by the citizens and the great ripple effect caused by public securement on the real economy, it can be considered as a naturally derived result.

Procurement operations are traditionally accompanied along with complicated procedures and various required documents, and are treated through frequent face-to-face contact. Not only was the probability of procurement corruption high between government workers and suppliers, but notices of bidding and results of successful bids were not displayed on a real time basis. This made it difficult to conduct effective surveillance or control for the procurement procedures, and conflicts regarding transparency and fairness often occurred.

During the year 2001 when KONEPS (Korean ON-line e-Procurement System) was constructed, the total procurement volume in Korea reached about KRW 67 trillion which accounted for about 47% of KRW 142 trillion won from the integrated financial scale[1], and had a great influence on the national economy and the private real economy. In this public procurement market, the securement of transparency through the display of diverse information about bidding announcement, procedures, and results and securement of fairness in selecting an appropriate supplier through proper competition were very important assignments which had to be completed.

....
1. The scale in which the expenditure budget of the central government such as the general accounts. special accounts. funds and special accounts of businesses in non-financial companies are combined.

(2) Increase in demand for the effectiveness of public procurement

The previously existing procurement administration was very ineffective as it was treated through complicated procedures, multiple documents, and face-to-face contacts. In the case of procurement suppliers, they had to participate in the bidding, and in order to conclude the procurement contract as the successful bidder, they had to issue documents one-by-one in the relevant institution. Additionally, they had to personally visit the requesting agency during each implementation stage of procurement, such as the participation in bidding, filling out contracts, making a request for examination on the inspection as well as payment. As a result, procurement suppliers consumed much time, manpower, and expenses in implementing the procurement.[2] The ineffectiveness also applied for the public institutions, which were the consumers. As the procurement processes relied on manual labor, this caused ineffectiveness in procurement administration. Furthermore, moral hazards such as public corruption occurred frequently in the field of procurement due to the inadequate display of information regarding the bidding, which led to ineffective surveillance and control of the procurement. These moral hazards led to ineffectiveness of public procurement.[3]

....

2. According to the "Study on analysis of operation effects for procurement informatization project and suggestion of development measures" conducted by the Korea Policy Institute in the year 2010, the cost reduction effect of the private sector (procurement business) made through the construction of the KONEPS was reported to reach up to 7.9 trillion won yearly.
3. Transparency International (TI) claimed that corruption and ineffectiveness in the public procurement division caused additional costs of more than USD 4000 billion dollars.

(3) Development of IT technology and the global trend of eProcurement

The rapid development of informational technology cannot be left out from the background to how eProcurement was realized. During the 1990s, each of the advanced countries were strengthened through the developed IT technology and focused on eProcurement as the reform measure of public procurement. Some countries actively introduced the eProcurement system.

Back then, the aspect which was most actively discussed between member nations of the GPA of WTO was on the application of information technology like the Internet. As a result, eProcurement stood out as a new paradigm which gained attention amongst world organizations, in addition to individual countries.

3) Construction process of the domestic eProcurement system

The completed version of the domestic eProcurement system can be considered to be KONEPS (Korean ON-line e-Procurement System, KONEPS)[4], which started its service from September 30th, 2002. The establishment of KONEPS was propelled by how multiple governmental institutions formed into a whole governmental consultative council. However, in actual terms, it was led by the PPS, which is the central procurement agency of Korea. The PPS accumulated the development and operation know-how

....
4. When KONEPS was first opened, its English title was GePS(Government electronic Procurement System), which was directly translated from Korean to English. However, after it was considered that the title would cause difficulties in providing national characteristics or differentiation, a contest was held in choosing its title. Therefore, its title was revised as KONEPS(Korea ON Line EProcurement Service) in October, 2006.

for the eProcurement system through the construction of the procurement EDI project and the electronic bidding system during the 1990s. In addition to the technological know-how by the PPS, the whole governmental support was one of the factors which enabled KONEPS to be successfully completed over a short period of time.

The process of constructing Korea's eProcurement system began with the EDI project propelled by the PPS in 1996, and was completed with KONEPS in 2002. The reason why the EDI project conducted in 1996 is considered to be the beginning of the eProcurement system is because KONEPS was constructed based on the technological foundation of the procurement EDI project.

(1) Procurement EDI Project (1996~2001)

EDI(Electronic Data Interchange) refers to the substitution of paper documents into electronic documents, and replacement of the traditional document delivery methods such as mail, phones, and in person with electronic documents. In Korea, the introduction of EDI began as it was first introduced to the field of trade and private and public institutions. When it was being introduced, it was recognized as an important measure which improved the high cost & ineffective structures applied by private businesses and public institutions.

The procurement EDI project set its objective to begin the implementation from 2001 and was propelled in-phases per each area of procurement administration. The first project stage, which took place from 1996 to 1997, introduced the EDI system to the fields which required major procurement (unit price contract) and revision of procurement requests (unit price contract) which require minor costs for system construction and display major effects. It is also a pilot stage where the governmental EDI support center system is constructed for the distribution of electronic documents. The second project stage is the diffusion stage which took place from 1998 to 2001. It stabilized the pilot system and expanded the operation to the targeted institutions (requesting agency & procurement supplier). The third project stage took the procurement EDI constructed from the first and second stages and implemented the system throughout all fields of procurement administration.

Table 3-2. The process of Procurement EDI establishment

Per stage		Intended Operation	Requesting agency (Total)	Information linkage center	Linked VAN
1st stage(1997) (Pilot operation)		Domestic goods (unit price contract)	20	Pilot operation	Insurance network Private VAN
2nd stage (Diffusion)	1998~1999	Domestic goods, (Non-stored & stored goods) Accountancy	500 (520)	Began preparation for EDI support	Private VAN, Financial network national defense procurement EDI
	2000~2001	purchasing of foreign goods, construction contracts	2,000 (2,520)	System expansion	Tariff network, Distribution network, industrial information network
3rd stage(2001 onward)		All implemented	All	All implemented	Foreign VAN

PPS applied the EDI to convert their system from relying on paper documents for procurement into an electronic document system. This allowed for the simplification & standardization of the procurement operations. As a result, this enhanced productivity and efficiency of procurement administration. The expense reduced annually back then through the EDI business was estimated to be about KRW 52 billion.

(2) Construction of the electronic bidding system (2000)

The introduction of an electronic bidding system similar to KONEPS in which the bids are transmitted through cyber space was attempted through the procurement EDI pilot project in 1997. However, the lack of recognition and insufficient regulations caused it to fail. Thus, it was propelled again through the procurement EDI diffusion project in the year 2000.

The electronic bidding system which started its construction since May 2000 opened a homepage called 'www.electronicbidding.go.kr' in November 2000 and began the electronic bidding service. As the enforcement decree of the national contract law became revised and applicable acts of electronic bidding were provided on January 2001 the following year, the electronic bidding system was newly born with its new name: called the GoBIMS (Government Bidding Integrated System).

The 'Government Bidding Integrated System' is a widely used system which can be utilized in other public institutions along with the PPS. Considering that it was not the single window of public procurement to be used by all public institutions, unlike KONEPS established in 2002, there

Table 3-3. Number of Public institutions using electronic bidding system

(Based on the end of March 2001)

Classification	goods		construction and services		Total	
	Number of contract	Participating suppliers	Number of contract	Participating suppliers	Number of contract	Participating suppliers
PPS	1,036	2,910	135	44,593	1,171	47,503
Public Institutions	16	66	14	1,783	30	1,849
Total	1,052	2,976	149	46,376	1,201	49,352

were limits in the application & expansion of electronic bidding. However, it contained great meaning by the fact that it was constructed as the fourth electronic bidding system in the world and propelled the electronic commerce in the public procurement market.

(3) Establishment of KONEPS (2001~2002)

The Government Bidding Integrated System which was constructed by the PPS in the year 2001 could be applied by other public institutions, but it could not function as the single window of public procurement. Back then, large procurement institutions such as the Defense Procurement Agency and the Korea Electric Power Corporation self-constructed the eProcurement system, and some other institutions also considered building eProcurment systems. In some institutions, the introduction of the eProcurement system was proven to be effective. However, since the single window of public procurement was not available, the procurement suppliers had to collect the bidding information from each institution and identify the bid announcement. When registering the business for participation in the bidding, related documents had to be issued for each case and submitted repeatedly to public institutions. Thus, great inconvenience and increase in expenses had to be encountered. The government recognized these problems and formed an integrated council with the Ministry of Strategy and Finance, the Ministry of Public Administration and Security, the Ministry of Knowledge Economy, and the PPS in order to promote the public procurement reform through the construction of the single window of public procurement, and propelled the construction of the governmental eProcurement service. The construction of KONEPS was processed in two stages including the 「Establishment of basic plans for G2B activation(2001.4~2002.1)」 and 「Construction of the Government eProcurement (G2B) system(2002.2~2002.12)」. The major contents of the establishment are listed as follows.

• Construction of the Single Window for Public Procurement

Before KONEPS was constructed, the procurement suppliers had to identify all of the public institution's bidding information through an official gazette, newspaper, or websites of the institutions, and in order to participate in the bidding, they had to register for a license per institution.

After KONEPS was launched, the national contract law was revised so that all bidding information was required to be registered in KONEPS. This provided all bidding information to the public through an online single window. Particularly, as bidding information of 7 institutions including the Defense Procurement Agency, which already possessed separate eProcurement systems, were publically integrated in real-time to

Figure 3-1. Revised contents of KONEPS as the single window for the public procurement

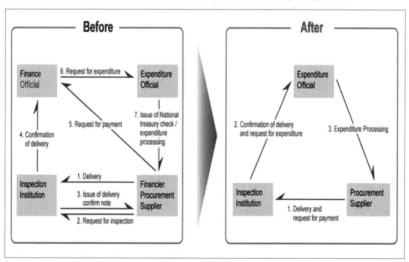

KONEPS. KONEPS was able to provide a complete service as the single window of public procurement. Since information of registered suppliers can be shared between public institutions, the suppliers can participate in all bidding of public institutions by only having to register once for bidding participation.

- Entire procurement processes from bidding to e-payment conducted online

Through integration with systems of other public institutions, KONEPS enabled documents needed for procurement processes such as the participation in bidding, qualification evaluation, and contracts which were to be confirmed online, and thoroughly simplified the procurement stages. Additionally, 166 related documents such as the bid, contract, request form for inspection and examination, and bill statement which were previously submitted through personal visits or mail became processed electronically. Consequently, the procurement business no longer needed to visit the government office, and the online processing of the procurement operation decreased the transaction costs of suppliers and increased the work efficiency.

(4) Reduction in time consumed for payment through revised procedures for payment

Operations such as the request for inspection and examination or confirmation of completion were processed online, and accounting operations were enabled through one system formed by the contract department, inspection department, and the expenditure department. As a result, the payment processes became thoroughly simplified, and the amount of time consumed for the payment was decreased significantly as well.

Figure 3-2. Revision of the payment procedures made by the KONEPS

Figure 3-2. Revision of the payment procedures made by the KONEPS

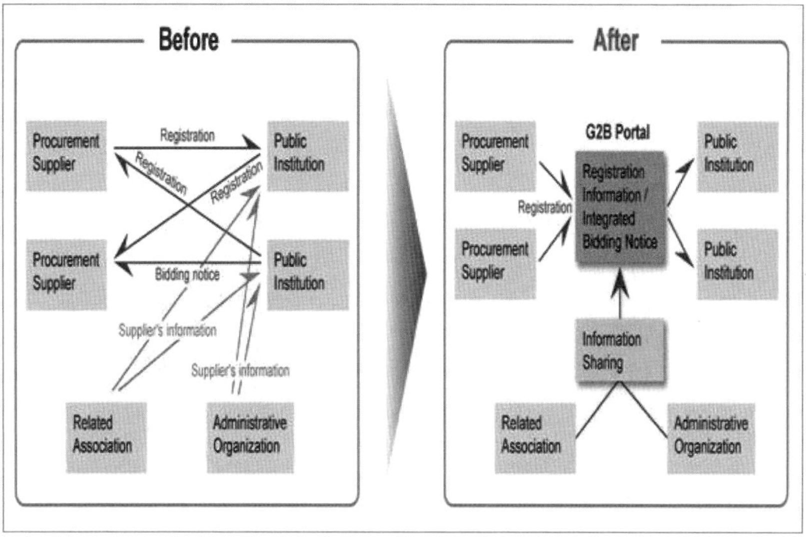

Because of the standardization of the classification system of government goods, which used to be operated differently per institution, the overlapping construction of the code system was eliminated.

Particularly, by converting the product classification system based on the UNSPSC classification system which is suitable for electronic commerce and strongly suggested by the UN, not only was the compatibility between private shopping malls and the international system endanced, but by applying various properties regarding individual products such as the specific standards, transaction conditions, and manufacturer data to fit the international standard, the qualitative expansion of product information was realized.

2. Legal & Systematic background for the introduction of eProcurement

As was mentioned earlier, the KONEPS is a single window of public procurement and is currently providing a one-stop service.

Before KONEPS was launched, the procurement suppliers had to spend a lot of time participating in public bidding as they had to confirm the bidding information through diverse forms of media such as the official gazette or newspaper, websites of each institution, or bulletin boards.

Table 3-4. Number of organizations using KONEPS

Division	Number of users		Transaction amount	Number of bidding
	Procurement supplier	Public institution		
2003	92,042	25,529	36 trillion won	99,020 cases
2011	218,719	43,708	64 trillion won	288,533 cases
Increase rate(%)	137.6%	71.2%	77.8%	191.4%

Thus, after KONEPS was opened, the bidding information of all public institutions could be checked through KONEPS. Not only this, but the procurement suppliers applied or registered to participate in bidding to the public institution for each bid, but since the system became available, the suppliers can now participate in bidding of all public institutions with a single registration. Furthermore, as KONEPS is integrating and processing the service with more than 50 other external systems and services, a one-stop service is being provided so that all operations starting from the bidding to the payment can be conducted within this system. After the opening in the year 2002, KONEPS is greatly increasing in the number of users and transaction amount and volume. Due to its successful operation, it has been receiving high evaluations from home and abroad.

The legal & systematic background to the successful introduction & operation of KONEPS is listed as follows.

1) Integrated efforts to set up the system

Considering the importance of public procurement, KONEPS couldn't cease by settling with a few institutions or specific operations. Instead, it

Figure 3-3. E-Government Committee to promote G2B systems

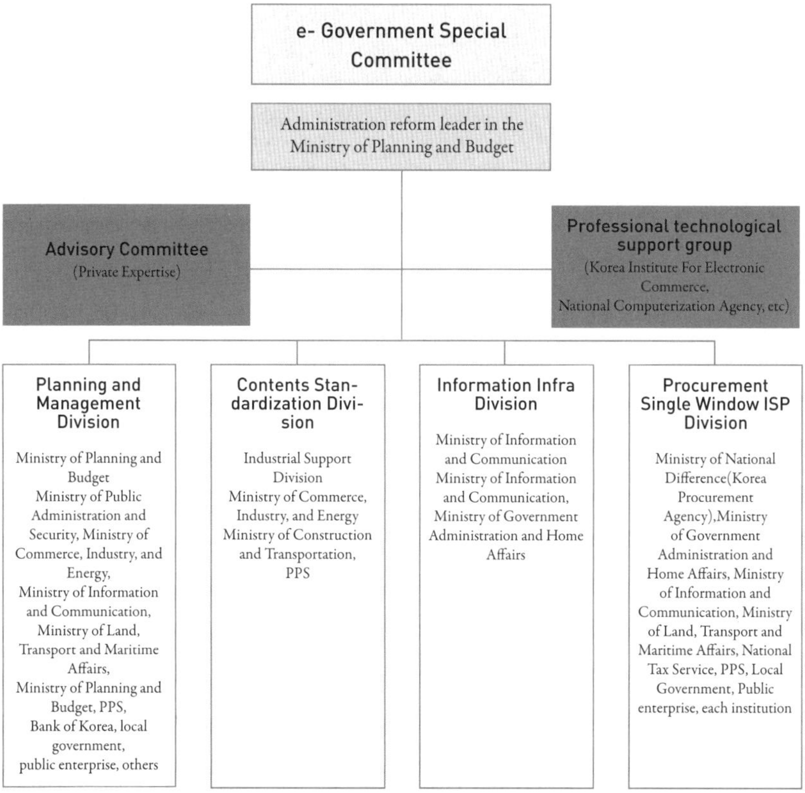

was a project to reform all the procurement administrations conducted by all public institutions. Each public institution had to reengineer the business process of the different procurement operations in an innovative manner, and an intimate cooperative body, e-Government committee, formed between the related authorities was considered as being important.

The first project stage (2001.4~2002.1) of KONEPS called the 'Establishment of information strategy planning for the KONEPS' assigned the Ministry of Planning and Budget as the leading institution and the Ministry of Information and Communication and the PPS were selected as the joint leading institutions and were propelled amongst the participation of

Figure 3-4. Collaborative body to launch KONEPS

e- Government Special Committee

Practical Promotion Manager
(PPS e-procurement Director General)
System Construction
Organization
Overall Control Organization
System and DB Construction Organization
Law . Institution Improvement Organization

G2B Support Conference
(Deputy Administrator of PPS)
Government Branch
The Ministry of Finance and Economy, Ministry of Education, Ministry of National Defense, Ministry of Public Administration and Security, Ministry of Commerce Industry and Energy, Ministry of Information and Communication, Ministry of Construction Transportation, Ministry of Planning and Budget, PPS, National Computerization Agency
G2B Consultation Platform
G2B Innovation Planning Establishment Service Advisory Panel

Review committee
Review committee
Organizations expected to use the system
Related organizations with external systems to be linked with the system

many ministries.

The 2nd project stage (2002.2~2002.12) of KONEPS began with designating the PPS as the single leading institution because of the short-term business plans and its system development history. Furthermore, just like the way the informatization strategy planning was established, the project was completed with collaborative efforts by many relevant authorities.

2) Legal Basis for the Implementation and promotion of the eProcurement

In order for eProcurement to be successfully introduced into the public field, an issue which is just as important as the actual system establishment is revising related legislations. For KONEPS, the revision of related legislation was progressed comparatively amicably. This was because there wasn't much to be amended from the existing legislation and the active participation of related fields was possible since the suppliers were promoted along with the legal system. As a result, all the legislations related to eProcurement were rearranged before the eProcurement services were commenced.

The information which is worth mentioning for the related legislation amendment is the ability to minimize the confusion which may be caused by the sudden introduction of eProcurement through interim measures. KONEPS began its eProcurement service on September 30, 2012 and executions were made to be identical to before by placing interim measures on some of the new functions until December 31, 2002. Therefore, they made sure that the procurement operation would not be suspended even for public institutions which were not ready to utilize KONEPS. As a result, public institutions were able to carry out procurement operations through the utilization of KONEPS thanks to the newly amended legislation since

September 30, 2002. Not only that but they were able to gain the time needed in utilizing KONEPS ordinarily while carrying out procurement operations according to previous procurement legislations.

Reviewing the revisions made in the legislation, the previous official gazettes, newspapers and public notices which are published in the homepages of separate public organizations were made compulsory to make announcements in the data-processing system(KONEPS). Furthermore, through making regulations to permit electronic bids but exclude offline bids, KONEPS was formed so that KONEPS public procurement would be able to function as a practical single window.

Additionally, the one stop service, which can confirm all procurement

Table 3-5. Legislative Revision for KONEPS

Legislations	Main Revision Details	Revision Period
National Contract Law Enforcement Ordinance	The notice of tenders which were dependent upon previous gazettes or newspapers were obligated to be listed on KONEPS The legal status of the electronic bidding was strengthened and electronic buildings which exclude offline bids but only permits electronic bids was permitted for enforcement The obligation for the utilization of KONEPS to announce the illegitimate manufacturers' information The obligation of overall contract records through the utilization of KONEPS The arrangement of applicable provisions based on the utilization of KONEPS	2002.7.30
National Contract Law Enforcement Regulations	The Arrangement of multi-access basis for suppliers by public organization, which are registered to KONEPS	2002.8.24
Local Finance Act Enforcement Ordinance	all the local tenders are obligated to be announced on KONEPS the notification of Illegitimate manufacturers were obligated to be listed on KONEPS to manage the suppliers' information systematically	2002.11.29

information from KONEPS at once, was made possible. Due to the compulsory registration of KONEPS by suppliers, if they have triggered contract defaults or illegal practices, they will have limited access to the bidding of the public organization for a certain period of time. Furthermore, the arrangement of applicable provisions was made possible for each public organization to have access to the illegitimate suppliers.

3. Systematic and Technological Background needed for the Introduction of the eProcurement system

1) Reorganization of groups & human resources for the reinforcement of eProcurement

Generally, the PPS was criticized for not forming a group system based on clear analysis about its position and role as the central procurement institution or attempting to apply it effectively.

It began as the 「Provisional Office of Foreign Supply」, an institution needed for the systematic and effective management of aid goods after South Korea was founded. Then, it went through transitions as the 「Office of Foreign Procurement」, 「Office of Foreign Supply Management」, 「Office of Foreign Supply」, and the 「PPS」, and it was able to add different functions needed to meet different situations.

However, with increasing demand for eProcurement internally and externally, the fundamental changes in organizational and personnel structure of PPS were needed to implement eProcurement effectively. As a result, the Public Procurement reinforced the function of eProcurement implementation and reduced other functions accordingly in order to restructure the organization.

When the informatization groups and workers before & after the opening of KONEPS between 1997 and 2004 are compared, the eProcurement divisions have been increased from 1 to 2 divisions, and the number of government workers who specialized in electronics increased from 15 to 23 workers, and the number of contracted workers increased by 45 personnel. The number of personnel from the eProcurement division increased compared to how the overall numbers of personnel in the PPS, which decreased from 1,083 to 944 personnel during the same period. This demonstrated how the PPS recognized eProcurement as the core function and concentrated on capability based on the systematic dimension for the construction and operation of the eProcurement system.

Table 3-6. Changes in organizational & personnel structure of PPS for the eProcurement ('97~'04)

eProcurement Development Stage	Status of exclusive division & numbers of personnel for eProcurement	Service level
1st stage of procurement EDI ('97~'00)	1st division(Information management division) Total of 15 government workers specializing in the electronics	Domestic goods & Part of the accounting operation utilizing workers within the organization
2nd stage of procurement EDI ('01~'02)	2nd division(Information planning division) Total of 19 government workers specializing in the electronics 13 personnel from external sources(contracted workers)	All internal tasks such as those related to the constructions works/foreign goods Electronic bidding, expansion of external service based on shopping malls used by 20,000 institutions and 70,000 businesses
KONEPS ('03~'04)	2nd division(Information planning division facilities) Total 23 government workers specializing in the electronics 45 personnel from external sources(non-government workers)	Informatization of all public procurement operations Single window of public procurement used by 30,000 institutions and 100,000 businesses

From the systematic dimension, attention should be given to the fact that an advanced outsourcing system was introduced to effectively manage KONEPS. As the use of KONEPS increased, the increasing amount of work could not be handled by the government worker in charge of internal informatization. Therefore, the outsourcing of informatization personnel from the private sector was considered necessary. However, reliance towards the personnel conducting the consigned operations was intensified during the outsourcing process and the professionalism of the government worker in charge of internal informatization declined. Furthermore, a problem was suggested as processing and control measures had to be reinforced on the consigned business implementing the core operations.

In the meantime, the maintenance contract method with the consigned business which only lasted for a year caused frequent changes in the outsourcing personnel, and the problem of not being able to secure continuity and stability in the system operation occurred. Additionally, since the consigned business didn't have motivating factors about service quality or improvements of functions, it was difficult to provide a prompt and appropriate service for the user demands. This resulted in complaints from the system's users.

In order to supplement the basic management system of the consigned business, the PPS introduced a new outsourcing model. A long term outsourcing contract system which supplemented the previous contract and calculation methods of the assigned personnel and reflected the technically upgraded unit cost was introduced. Moreover, a contract which deals with the prearranged Service Level Agreement (SLA[5]) instead of assigned personnel was concluded and a new outsourcing model was established.

· · · · · · · ·
5. SLA - Agreement which may charge the penalty or give incentives to a contractor depending on the performance.

Table 3-7. Improvements in KONEPS operation consignment system

Classification	Previous	Improvement
Contract formation	1 year contract Fixed price(all operation), No payment provided for additional development	Continuous long term contract(3 years) Fixed price(basic maintenance) Price fluctuation(additional improvement operations)
Calculation for the amount of work	Calculation of the amount of work according to the personnel expenditure	Calculation of clear amounts of work based on tasks
Service management	Service management system is non existent	SLA based service management

A 3 year long term contract was introduced through the initiation of the new outsourcing method. Through this, stability of personnel operation was made possible, and a staged service improvement was even enabled each year.

Moreover, as compensation was distributed to the amount of work conducted by the consigned business by introducing the variety cost system in which payments are calculated to the fixed payment following the additional operation, this induced consigned businesses to bring voluntary improvements to the provided service. Not only this, but by managing contracts based on the level of service quality, system operations became stabilized and the service quality was enhanced.[6]

2) Construction of IT infra and development of technology for electronic commerce system

....
6. The new consigned operation model received positive evaluations as it was even introduced as an outstanding case in the "Whole governmental debate for the creation of the environment which recognizes SW value" held in March 24th, 2006 under the chairmanship of then-President.

(1) Construction of the IT infra at a national level

When the eProcurement system was introduced to the public sector during the periods of the late 1990s to the beginning of 2000, our domestic IT industries were able to achieve rapid developments. The former president Kim Dae Joong had great interest in building a powerful IT nation as he identified his vision during his inauguration in the year 1998 and how he would 'create a powerful intelligent nation by developing Korea into a country which globally excels in computer utilization'.

Until the year 1998, the number of domestic users of high-speed Internet was only around 14,000 users, and our country had a very low IT standard. Back in those days, most people relied on PC communication using telephone lines, and most citizens were even unfamiliar even with this communication method and considered it difficult to approach. However, Korea became influenced by the active IT industry promotion during the presidency of President Kim Dae Joong, and our IT infra developed into an IT infra at the level of developed countries within a short period of time. The immense growth of the IT industry which took place during the 5 years of the presidency of Kim Dae Joong can also be verified through numerical representations. Compared to how the number of households which registered for high-speed Internet, which consisted of only 14,000 households in the year 1997, it increased by more than 700 times, and 10,400,000 households were registered by the year 2002[7]. Additionally the number of people who use the Internet increased from 1,630,000 users to 2,627,000 users and recorded a rapid increase.[8]

....
7. The fact that 1,040,000 households are registered for the Internet statistically refers to how an internet connection is supplied for each 4 people households and those who have a computer can easily use the Internet from their homes.

Table 3-8. Internet supply and growth in IT industries during the period of President Kim Dae Joong's presidency

Classification	1997	2002
Number of households registered for internet	14,000 households	1,040,000 households
Number of internet users	1,630,000 users	2,627 users
IT industry productivity	76 trillion won	189 trillion won

Furthermore, in accordance to the Internet propagation, the amount of production reached up to KRW 189 trillion won in 2002, and the share of GDP also expanded from 8.6% in the year 1998 to 14.9% in the year 2002. This is a numerical value which overtook America (11.1%) and Japan (9.6%) during the same time period.

The development in domestic IT industries took place rapidly and was globally unprecedented. It formed social conditions in which the Internet can be used at all times and places and activated the application of electronic commerce between private sectors. It also opened the way for the domestic electronic government. As a result, an opportunity was provided for the eProcurement system to be introduced to the public sector in a stable manner.

Even back in those days, a clear social agreement existed about eProcurement being an important reform measure for public procurement, but if a national IT infra was not properly constructed based on eProcurement, it would have been difficult for the domestic public procurement system to be introduced successfully.

. . . .
8. After being strengthened by the active Internet supply policy during the presidency of President Kim DaeJoong, the domestic Internet supply rate was reported as 70.5% by the year 2006 and was leading other major developed countries such as US, Japan, and Canada.

(2) Application of the latest technology to secure the safety of electronic commerce

Since the eProcurement system processes all procedures starting from the bid notice of goods, services and construction which cost from tens of millions of won to billions of won, the safety of the system and securement of reliability are very important.

When the eProcurement system was first introduced, eProcurement was recognized as the core reform measure of procurement administration, but it is true that there were great concerns about security issues and the safety of online procurement operation processes. From the perspective of the procurement suppliers, they started to become anxious about their bidding amount or personal information being exposed. This was because the system changed from bids submitted after being personally written and enclosed to bids being sent through electronic documents. In terms of the PPS which operated the eProcurement system, extreme caution had to be given to the system's security and safety since all procurement stages are processed online and severe damage or errors in the system can lead to major disasters.

KONEPS applied the electronic signature of the PKI[9] method and the document security technology in order to secure the safety of electronic commerce. The end-to-end security system based on electronic documents was established by applying the official electronic signatures to all operations from producing & transmitting the electronic document from the sender's PC and registering them onto the receiver's PC. Additionally, in the case of the bidding, a 'national authorized password algorithm' man-

....
9. PKI (Public Key Infrastructure) : Infrastructure where transmitters & receivers access for certifications and others with using encrypted keys

aged by a new key for every bidding was used to increase security. With a PKI based system, not only does it become issued from the National Information Society Agency, but the person in charge of the operation can store and manage it. This made it impossible for even the system operator to check it. If the person in charge lost it, they had to follow the fixed procedures and submit a request for reissuing from the PPS, and the PPS had to submit a request for reissuing from the National Information Society Agency. This enabled the construction of a firm security system.

Meanwhile, the PPS installed a dual firewall, in which the main server and network were physically separated, and a data backup system to provide the non-stop service which was available 24 hours/365 days in preparation for possible system errors. The objective of the backup system was set as 'being able to restore the data which existed shortly before the occurrence of the disaster within 4 hours.' In order to accomplish this goal, the system was constructed in the form of a mirror web site. The backup support center has been installed in a joint government backup center located in Yong-in, Gyeonggi-do. With this center, service can be restored within 4 hours even if problems occur in the main operation system.

KONEPS provided a stable eProcurement system by applying thorough security policies and increased reliability for the operation of the system. These accomplishments provided the opportunity to enhance public reliability in eProcurement.

4. Worker empowerment for the introduction of the eProcurement system

The introduction of the eProcurement system not only consists not only of changes in which procurement operations are processed with computers connected to the internet. Additionally, it carries behavioral changes in which advancement is made from previous customs, and the operations are processed through new methods. Therefore, worker empowerment strengthened through the acquisition of new technology and appropriate behavioral changes can be considered a key factor in the successful stability and utilization in the eProcurement system.

1) Worker empowerment for operators of the eProcurement system

Through the establishment of the procurement EDI business and the opening and operation of the GoBIMS implemented by the PPS before KONEPS was opened in the year 2002, outstanding information and workers were secured. By taking the lead in implementing the procurement information business compared to other public institutions, it was able to attain the most outstanding informative workers amongst public institutions in the dimension of eProcurement. The securement of the outstanding informative workers became the base for the successful construction of KONEPS, which was completed over a short period of time.

After opening KONEPS, the PPS improved its appointed system to strengthen the workers in charge of informatization. Compared to how the workers in charge of informatization only worked in specific information divisions such as the information planning division and information management division, a rotational appointment system was introduced so that a worker could be transferred to another division after a certain period of time. With the system implemented, the worker was not limited to the dimension of the system operator, but was enabled to view the operation from the perspective of the system users. This widened workers' view of the operation increased the comprehensibility of the procurement operations.

2) Empowerment of competence for users of the eProcurement system

In order to minimize the initial confusion which could possibly occur during the opening of KONEPS, the PPS implemented training for users of KONEPS through various methods.

In terms of the applied methods, group training and cyber education were both applied. Particularly, the Electronic Commerce Resource Center under the Ministry of Commerce, Industry and Energy which is located nationwide was used to implement omnidirectional educational training. Moreover, in case of the large public institutions which possess training centers, visiting educators were provided.

For the training of call-center agents of KONEPS, an intense training program was processed over a period of 1 month based on contents including the systematic functions and practical operations of KONEPS as well as FAQ by KONEPS system users.

5. New assignments of the eProcurement and solution measures

KONEPS, which was initiated in the year 2002 is considered one of the most outstanding examples amongst Korea's electronic governments. Through overthrowing the irrational customs of the procurement administration and digitalizing all procurement procedures, the transparency and effectiveness of the procurement administration made a groundbreaking development. Through these outcomes, KONEPS was evaluated as the highest leveled public electronic procurement system not only domestically but also internationally.

In modern times, the IT environment is going through vast changes which can be considered as fast as the speed of a thought. The administration environment which surrounds public procurement is also undergoing rapid changes. In order for KONEPS to maintain its brand value as the leading electronic procurement system, there is a need to seek an active solution for the challenges which are derived from changes.

1) Construction of private & public business platform with the increase in demands for electronic procurement

As government expenditures have been expanded in recent times, the transparent procurement for nonprofit organizations like property management offices which receive government subsidies, are gaining more social interest.[10] In particular, for small scale private organizations which cannot develop self electronic procurement systems, demand in the utilization of KONEPS is increasing.[11]

As was mentioned earlier, KONEPS increased fairness and efficiency

....
10. When procurement corruption connected to property management offices continued, the Ministry of Land, Transport, and Maritime Affairs obligated competitive bidding for the selection of construction or service businesses worth more than KRW 2 million won by the property management office starting from July, 2009 (Ministry of Land, Transport, and Maritime Affairs 'Guidelines to selecting property management contractors or businesses').
11. The PPS requested the Research Lab, a professional public survey business, to conduct a survey on the public's intentions of using KONEPS. They targeted on property management offices and private businesses as the subjects. As a result, 60% of property management offices and 54.5% of private businesses had the inclination to use KONEPS.

and made innovative improvements to the procurement administration. Until now, suppliers faced limitations when utilizing KONEPS. However, when considering the user demands for electronic procurement, open and flexible policies must be arranged in order for private interests to also be able to utilize KONEPS.

If KONEPS, which can only be utilized by government offices, is developed into a new business platform which both the public and private sector can use, the innovative outcome produced by KONEPS in the field of public procurement can be expanded into a social innovation throughout all areas of the society. Opening KONEPS to the private sector will enable the private businesses to make purchases through the system. This will be one of the most important assignments for KONEPS to face with in the days ahead.

2) Provision of the Smart Procurement Service based on the Spreading of Mobile Devices

As the application of mobile devices have been institutionalized after welcoming the era of 3 thousand million smartphone users, the demand for BYOD(Bring Your Own Device) and other mobile services is increasing.[12] In case of KONEPS, mobile service is at a low level in comparison to the web service. Therefore, it is evaluated to have the necessity for improvement in the mobile service.

In order to increase the level of mobile electronic procurement services, mobile applications and mobile webs must be established and supplied in the short term. However, in the long run, KONEPS must be restructured

....
12. According to the Korea Communications Commission, the number of domestic smartphone users has been reported as 31,410,000 in October, 2012.

overall based on HTML5, which is the standard web of the next generation. Additionally, an electronic procurement system which can be utilized freely without being bound up by devices and operation systems must be established.

3) Strategic Informatization of Procurement Data based on the Big Data Era

As we have recently approached the web 3.0 era in which a new fusion of knowledge is being created, big data is rising as the new topic in the IT industry, and the competition to gain the leadership of big data is becoming more fierce. Major developed countries such as the US and the UK are gaining more interests for big data, and they are even increasing the advantages to public service and implementing public data collection and analytical businesses.

KONEPS is an enormous cyber system applied by more than 200,000 procurement suppliers and more than 40,000 public institutions, and massive procurement data of more than 280,000 electronic bids are being accumulated annually. Thus, due to the lack in awareness about big data and the absence of a systematic data management system, the massive amount of procurement data being accumulated in KONEPS are not being managed adequately.

In order to apply procurement data as strategic information needed for the improvement of the procurement service, a big data management system should be constructed in order for a virtuous cycle of "Accumulation of procurement data $\rightarrow$ Operation application $\rightarrow$ Service improvement $\rightarrow$ Accumulation of procurement data" to be formed.

4) Provision of security measures for the increase in cyber threats

As mentioned earlier, there were great concerns about cyber security before KONEPS was introduced. Thus, the PPS applied effective security technology to KONEPS and eliminated this area of concern. Still, a new type of cyber threat continued as eProcurement became generalized. In order to effectively cope against cyber threats which seem to become more intellectualized, it is most important to pre-estimate the security problems and prepare security measures which can act against these situations. For instance, the Fingerprint Recognition e-Bidding System, which was introduced as the world's first system by the PPS to block the source of illegal online rigged bids between procurement businesses, was an exemplary case of an anticipative security measure.

6. Conclusion: Implication and Suggestion

This case study identified the policies of eProcurement and the legal, systematic, organizational, technological backgrounds of eProcurement relevant to the domestic public sector. Moreover, challenges encountered by eProcurement as well as solution measures have been examined.

Unlike how the private sector introduced eProcurement with the aim of the economical value of improvement in efficiency, the public sector focused on the moral values such as fairness and transparency instead of efficiency when promoting the introduction of eProcurement.

KONEPS (Korean ON-line e-Procurement System), which was constructed in the year 2002, dispelled all of the concerns suggested during the first introduction of the system, and is currently receiving outstanding evaluations as it was even recognized as the 'best practice' of electronic government in domestic and foreign areas. By displaying all public sector procurement procedures on a real-time basis, the public procurement administration, which was recognized to have a negative image due to corruption, was reformed in addition to extensive improvements made in the effectiveness of task processing through the eProcurement operations.

The reason why KONEPS was able to display a phenomenal increase in fairness and effectiveness in procurement administration and succeed as the best domestic global eProcurement model was due to how KONEPS took on the role as the single window of public procurement in South Korea.

Currently, as 10 years have passed since first opening in the year 2002, KONEPS has been able to achieve an outstanding performance. However, it still encounters numerous challenges. The IT environment surrounding KONEPS is drastically changing, and the standards of customers using eProcurement are continuously increasing. In order for KONEPS to continue developing its current status, continuous changes and efforts for innovation will be essential. While integrating the newest IT advances to provide a service which is suitable for the increasing standards of the customers, active countermeasures will be needed against security threats such as hacking or leakage of information in order to support a stable service.

Note: This article was funded by and reported to Korea Eximbank in 2012.

References

Korea Association of Purchase Procurement. (2002). 2002 Spring Symposium of the Korea Association of Purchase Procurement. *Presentation material of Korea Association of Purchase Procurement.*

Korea Policy Evaluation Institute. (2010).*A study on the analysis of operation effects in the procurement information business and development measures.*

Public Procurement Service. (2008).*60 year history of the PPS.*

Public Procurement Service. (2009). *eProcurement e-book.*

Public Procurement Service. (2012). *Future strategies 2017 for eProcurement.*

Public Procurement Service. (2012). *Procurement statistics.*

Seoul National University. (2000). *Development measures for the procurement administration which is in accordance to the eCommerce era.*

Song, Hee-jun. (2003). *Performance of administration reform through the eProcurement and future direction.*

Chapter 4

Introduction of Tax Administration Information System (TAMIS)

Yunhi Won (University of Seoul)

Introduction of Tax Administration Information System (TAMIS)

Yunhi Won (University of Seoul)

1. Policies

Computerization of tax administration in Korea has been continuously carried out gradually as step-by-step process since the establishment of the National Tax Administration(NTA) in 1966. The first mainframe computer was purchased in 1970, and computerized data processing was initiated. The basic framework of the current system was constructed with the introduction of the Tax Integrated System(TIS) in 1997. Since then, many new systems have been introduced, including the homepage of the NTA in 1999, the Home Tax Service(HTS) in 2002, the Tax Information Management System(TIMS) in 2003, the Cash Receipt Service System in 2005, the Tax Law Information System in 2007, the Electronic Tax Invoice System in 2010, etc. And a 'New-Generation TIS' has been under construction since 2012.

The NTS(2006) classified informatization process of the Korean tax administration from 1967 to 2006 into 6 periods as follows: (1)the preparation period for introducing computer hardware (1967~1971); (2)the development period of the tax data processing system (1971~1981); (3)the expansion period of tax data processing in terms of its areas and functions (1982~1992); (4)the period of tax administration reform centered on TIS development (1993~1996); (5)the period of take-off towards scientific tax administration and of setting the foundation of e-taxation (1997~2000); and (6)the period of advanced e-taxation fit for the 21st century (2001~). The four major developments in the Korean e-taxation are explained as follows:

1) Automated Data Processing

The earliest form of the Korean e-taxation initiative began in 1970 as a form of automated data processing. The NTA purchased a mainframe computer for the first time and established the electronic data processing center. During the following 10 years the NTA tried to enhance scopes of electronic data processing with a batch-mode system to increase efficiency of tax data processing.

During the 1980s two Five-Year Plans of Informatization of Tax Administration were implemented. At this stage, more emphasis was put on expanding scopes of computer utilization for taxation. In 1985, the NTA constructed a master database from which data could be accessed and retrieved at regional and branch offices through a direct network built on communication line. In 1987, the NTA began to provide personal computers to tax officers, and reached the goal of 1 PC per staff member in 1997.

The early form of data processing, that is, electronic data input, creation of tax data base, and data operation had been gradually transformed into data management. With the introduction of TIS, tax data was merged, accumulated and analyzed for various purposes. For example, TIMS introduced in 2003 made it possible to systematically analyze accumulated data and utilize the information for various decision making, such as tax base management and tax auditing.

2) Tax Integrated System(TIS)

In 1997 TIS was installed after three years and four months of a construction period with costs of around US60 million. The project was originally initiated to prepare for processing huge data transactions expected to occur due to the enactment of the Real Name Transaction of Financial Assets Act in 1993 and the comprehensive taxation of financial income afterwards.

Since its inception, TIS has been the main data management system of the Korean e-taxation. It drastically changed business environments of NTA. First, it was built in accordance with the functional structure of NTA, such as filing, auditing, collection, and taxpayer service, which made it easier to implement organizational reform in 1999. Second, all tax offices were connected through WAN and LAN in on-line real time mode. Third, many new internal systems such as the electronic mailing system, electronic documentation system, intranet system for knowledge sharing, and electronic bulletin board were introduced in accordance with TIS to enhance the efficiency of tax administration.

In 2000, the Submission and Management of Taxation Data Act was enacted and thereby expanded the scope of tax data to be reported to the National Tax Service(NTS). In fact, government departments and agencies had been expected to submit tax-related data to tax authorities by the prime minister's ordinance since 1975, but the impact had been limited. The 2000 Act expanded the scope of related organization and data to be submitted. In addition to governmental departments and agencies, financial institutions and public entities were included, and they were to submit all taxation-related data, such as registration, permission, contract, payment, and tax invoice, etc.

In 2003 the Tax Information Management System(TIMS) was established to utilize TIS data for tax enforcement purposes. It has provides an in-depth analysis of tax data for decision makings at different levels of tax offices.

The TIS of 1997, however, has been repeatedly patched up to reflect numerous changes in tax laws and policies, with separate systems having been installed with new laws and policies, which resulted in duplicated data storage and compatibility problems. Moreover, the TIS of 1997 adopted the closed system of the IBM mainframe and it was difficult to cope with Unix-based open systems. "Next-Generation TIS" has been reviewed and proposed by NTS for more than a decade now, since 2004.

3) Home Tax Service (HTS)

(1) Background and Development Process

In 1999 the National Tax Administration carried out a reform on a large scale, called 'The 2nd Opening of NTS'. A key direction of the reform was creating a taxpayer-focused organization that emphasized taxpayer services. For example, the Taxpayer Service Center was established to provide one-stop services to taxpayers, and the English name of the organization was changed from National Tax Administration to National Tax Sesvice(NTS). The reform in 1999 greatly enhanced the level of taxpayer services, but NTS services still operated on an office-visit and direct-contact basis. In other words, taxpayers still had to visit tax offices and submit hardcopy or handwritten documents. Moreover, taxpayers and tax officials had to meet in person to deal with various tax matters.

The HTS changed the characteristics of the NTS service from the visit-based to on-line based one. In 2001, the HTS project was selected as one of 11 key projects of e-Government, which made it easier to secure the necessary budget.

(2) Major Features of the HTS

First, the electronic filing of 9 national taxes was made possible. These are income tax, corporation tax, VAT, withholding tax, individual consumption tax, liquor tax, securities transaction tax, stamp tax, and education tax. Taxpayers can type in their tax returns directly on the screen or use eligible tax accounting software. Taxpayers can get tax credits for HTS filing, which have been about U$9 for VAT, and U$18 for income tax and corporation tax.

Second, the electronic invoicing service of national taxes is provided to those who registered for the service. the NTS notifies tax invoice through email or text messages, then taxpayers can check the invoice on the system.

Third, taxpayers can pay their tax dues to the HTS through a bank transfer or by credit card. Taxpayers need to pay a convenience fee for credit card payments. Taxpayers can print electronic payment certificate using their home printers and can use it for official purposes.

Fourth, taxpayers can process various tax affairs with the NTS through the HTS. 144 out of 240 tax affairs that the NTS deals with can be processed through the system. And 11 certificates such as business registration, temporary close of business, and tax payment records can be issued through the system. Because anti-forgery technology was developed and incorporated into the system in 2004, taxpayers can print those certificates at home and can use them for official purposes. Moreover, reporting of various tax data required by tax laws can also be carried out through the system.

Fifth, taxpayers can check their own information on taxes filed and/or paid. Taxpayers can calculate their tax dues in the HTS for capital gains tax, gift tax, and individual consumption tax for car purchase.

4) Simplified Year-end Tax Settlement System

The Simplified Year-end Tax Settlement System began its service in 2006. Before the system was introduced, wage and salary earners needed to submit various tax documents to claim income deductions and tax credits when they submitted settlements on their income tax payments at the end of the year. Expenditure records on medical expenses, insurance premiums, tuition payments, and credit/debit card receipts are some examples of the documents they needed to submit. Such paperwork had been very burdensome to taxpayers because they had to contact banks, hospitals, credit card companies, and other service providers to obtain receipts or summary reports issued specifically for tax settlement purposes.

After the system was introduced, taxpayers could get the necessary information by accessing their records in the system, and then submit them to claim tax credits and deductions. Taxpayers just need to check and submit them to their employers who collect all settlement files from their employees and turn them in to tax authorities. All institutions that had tax-related transactions with taxpayers had to report relevant tax data directly to the NTS. Taxpayers' tax filing, in fact, has been turning into a kind of formal ceremony in the sense that the tax authority possesses almost all information necessary for taxation, and tax filing is just like an act of confirmation on pre-filled documents.

The NTS is now providing a paperless tax return service. Taxpayers do not have to print expenditure records or tax documents anymore. Because all relevant information is already stored in the system, taxpayers retrieve and attach it to the tax return in a file format.

2. Legal and Institutional Background

The legal and institutional aspects of informatization of tax administration are twofold. First, tax administration is the process through which the tax relations between taxpayers and tax authorities set by tax laws and decrees are realized. Therefore it has a significant impact on rights and duties of taxpayers, which is the reason why firm legal grounds are required for collecting, processing and publicizing taxpayers' information. Second, informatization of tax administration involves construction of very sophisticated and large-scale systems, which in turn requires large amount of financial resources. South Korea's experience indicates that financing such large-scale projects would be more acceptable when a community needs a fundamental reform.

Resident Registration Number(RRN) has been a key social infrastructure in Korea since the 1960's. RRN is a 13 digit identification number that contains information on birth date, sex, birth place, etc. Such an identification system is crucial to developing data and information systems because systems can be connected and merged by the number.

The Framework Act on Informatization Promotion of 1995 that was revised into the Framework Act on National Informatization in 2009 has laid the foundation for initiating various ICT projects. The purpose of the law was described as "to promote the informatization and lay the foundation for the ICT industry and achieve the advanced ICT industry infrastructure, thereby improving the life quality of people and contributing to growth of the national economy".

The Tax Integrated System (TIS) was originally initiated with the execution of the Real Name Financial Transaction System enacted by the Presidential Emergency Decree of August 12, 1993, and with implementation of the comprehensive taxation of financial incomes afterwards. Such institutional changes generated huge amount of taxation data related with financial transactions, thereby causing a large burden on the tax information system that was already over-tasked. The development of a new system could not be put off anymore.

Even though a large amount of taxation related data, such as taxpayers' basic information, income tax data, withholding tax data, and financial income data, etc, had been collected for the TIS, its scopes were still limited because the legal basis of the data collection was not firm and concrete enough. After the Act on the Submission and Management of Taxation Data of 2000 was enacted, the range of reporting institutions and the scope of data to be reported have expanded greatly. In addition to governmental departments and agencies, reporting institutions was expanded to include financial institutions and government-funded institutions.

The data they should submit to tax authorities includes those that has direct connection with the imposition and collection of the national taxes. Those pieces data are as follows: (1)data in issuing or getting authorization, permission, patent, registration, recording, reporting, etc., pursuant to laws; (2)data on the results of investigations and inspections conducted in accordance with laws; (3)data on the performance of operation, sales, production, and works, etc. that are reported in accordance with laws; (4) sum table of tax invoices and invoices issued or received pursuant to the VAT Act, the Income Tax Act, and the Corporation Tax Act; (5)data on the various types of subsidies, insurance benefits, mutual benefits payments that the submitting institutions pay and data on the business performance of members of some public organizations or institutions, etc.; (6)data kept by some central agencies and within the range of agreement between the NTS and chiefs of the agencies for the tax data management.

The Framework Act on National Taxes was amended in 1999 to incorporate electronic filing as one type of legitimate tax filings. Electronic filing is defined as a tax return made by means of the national tax information and communications networks of document related to returns pursuant to tax laws.

And the Digital Signature Act of 1999 was to establish the basic framework for digital signaturing. It aimed to strengthen security and reliability of electronic documents and to promote their usage, thereby stimulating use of electronic records and communications and advancing social benefit and convenience. Electronic transactions, such as tax filing, payments, and issuing tax certificates, are made legally possible owing to this Act.

The government have actively implemented government-wide e-Government initiatives since May 2001. A Special Committee on e-Government was established to promote and organize various e-Government projects. Home Tax Service(HTS) was selected as one of 11 key e-Government projects. Laws and regulations relating to electronic filing were aligned, and various filing forms were simplified fit to electronic filing. 'The Framework Act on National Taxes' was amended again in 2002 to incorporate various system changes, such as adjusting electronic delivery methods.

Another initiative for upgrading the e-taxation systems focusing a successful implementation of HTS was again selected as one of key 31 e-Government projects that the new government chose through its Presidential Committee on Government Innovation and Decentralization in 2004. Since its launch in 2002 the participation rate of HTS has remained low. Many remedies were introduced to promote taxpayers' utilization of HTS such as electronic filing. In order to make it easier to register into the HTS system, for example, Personal Identification Number(PIN) was mailed to taxpayers who did not have any authorized certificate. Tax credit for electronic filing and a new service of electronic issuing of tax documents were also introduced. Protection of personal information needs to be assured to promote taxpayers' involvement. NTS has prevented third parties from accessing documents by introducing an official certification procedure, excluding sensitive personal information like the name of a disease from documents, and recognizing taxpayers' right to refuse data provision and allowing taxpayers to remove data submitted. Owing to much effort to protect personal information, no data leakage has been reported since the NTS initiated the protection service in 2006.

Table 4-1. shows the proportion of tax returns filed electronically through HTS. We can see that almost all of Corporation Tax and withholding taxes are filed electronically. However, less than 80 percent of VAT filing is done electronically, which seems to reflect the existence of many small businesses.

Table 4-1. Proportion of Tax Returns Filed Electronically (Unit: %)

	Value Added Tax	Global Income Tax	Corporation Tax	Withholding Tax
2002	17.6	-	-	60.8
2003	33.8	43.5	92.7	78.9
2004	60.3	74.3	97.1	84.6
2005	75.4	81.2	96.9	88.4
2006	78.9	80.1	96.9	92.7
2007	75.1	80.7	96.1	93.3
2008	74.1	80.0	96.0	93.3
2009	74.6	83.4	96.1	96.1
2010	79.0	87.3	97.3	98.2

*Source: National Tax Service (each year).

3. Organizational and Technical Background

The TIS of 1997 connects the mainframe system of the headquarter office to those at regional and branch offices through exclusive networks, making it possible to put in and retrieve tax data directly at the front end terminals. The host computer of the headquarter office has been the IBM mainframe with which both on-line job and off-line batch job are executed. During daytime working hours it operats in on-line mode, and during night, backups and batch jobs are executed. At regional and branch offices medium- and small- sized workstation comprise the system that was shared among tax officials through LAN.

Contrary to the previous tax-based system, the main data base has been constructed in a function-based mode, including taxpayer registration, filing, and auditing, etc, which made it easier to reform the NTA organization from a tax-based to function-based one in 1999. And tax information accumulated and reproduced through the system has been organized by an individual taxpayer identified with resident registration number and address, which has enabled tax authorities to do the taxpayer's sincerity test easily. Table 4-2. compares characteristics of TIS and the previous system.

The NTA Reform in 1999 was a full-scale fundamental reform to be called as 'the 2nd Opening of NTS'. The reform focused on enhancing taxpayer services and preventing corruption of tax officials. Streamlining and transforming the NTA organization from a tax-based one to a function-based one, securing more personnel for taxpayer services and auditing functions, and establishing an office of taxpayer protection were main features of the reform.

But even after the 1999 reform the tax administration operated in a basically visit-based mode. Taxpayers had to visit tax offices directly and submit

Table 4-2. Comparison Systems of TIS and the previous one

Classification	Previous System	TIS
Network Connection	Computer to computer Connection of terminal at field offices to the mainframe at the head office	System to system Connection between systems of the head office and regional and field offices through network
Scope of Informatization	Processing taxation data	Informatization of tax offices
DB Composition	Tax-based DB 32 screens	Function-based DB 2,155 screens
Data input	Batch mode input by computer center	Input at field offices and electronically transmit
Data Processing	Batch job at the head office	Both on-line and batch mode
Data Output	Batch output and deliver to field offices	Output at field offices or on terminal

*Source: NTS (2006)

tax documents in a hardcopy format in order to deal with their tax matters. Tax officials also found much comfortable to meet taxpayers in person and have a face-to-face talk. HTS was selected as one of key e-Government projects in 2002 and would fundamentally transform the way the tax administration handled various tasks, such as tax filing and payment.

Since 2004, the NTS has tried to overhaul their entire informatization system to reflect the changing environments of tax administration and technology, and develop a new-generation TIS. As shown in Figure 4-1., the current system consists of 16 systems for internal use and 9 systems for the taxpayer service, and 426 servers and 828 application software applications. Then Figure 4-2. shows the whole conceptual framework of the system around the TIS.

The reason why the system is so complex is that when new functions or

Figure 4-1. The System Structure of e-Taxation of NTS (2011)

e- Government Special Committee		Taxpayer Service (9 Systems)	Government Business in Common (3 System)

Key Internal Business Support (10 Systems)	Major Internal Business Support (2 Systems)

Key Internal Business Support (10 Systems)

- Tax Integrated System (TIS)
- Tax Information Management System (TIMS)
- Audit Information System
- Foreign Currency Integrated Information System
- Integrated Tax Analysis System of International Trade
- Delinquent Management System
- Early Notification System of Credit Card Transaction
- Tax Data Submission and Management System
- VAT Tax Base Management System
- Electronic Library System

Major Internal Business Support (2 Systems)

- Electronic Document System
- Knowledge Management System

Other Internal Business Support (4 Systems)

- Integrated Performance Management System
- Internal Audit Management System
- Cyber Education System
- Capacity Evaluation System

Taxpayer Service (9 Systems)

- NTS Homepage
- Home Tax Service (HTS)
- Cash Receipt Registration System
- Simplified Year-End Settlement System
- EITC System
- Customer Satisfaction System
- Tax Law Information System
- Policy PR System
- Electronic Invoice System

Government Business in Common (3 System)

- e-Human
- Government Business Management System
- Public Officials' Wealth Registration System

Support of Informatization (6 Systems)

- IT Business Management Portal
- Service Capacity Management System
- IT Specialist Education Management System
- Integrated Software Management System
- Integrated Security System
- Network Management System

*Source: Korea Development Institute, Overhaul of the IRS Information System for Supporting Financial Sustainability, a preliminary feasibility study report, 2011

Figure 4-2. System Structure of the Korea e-Taxation around TIS

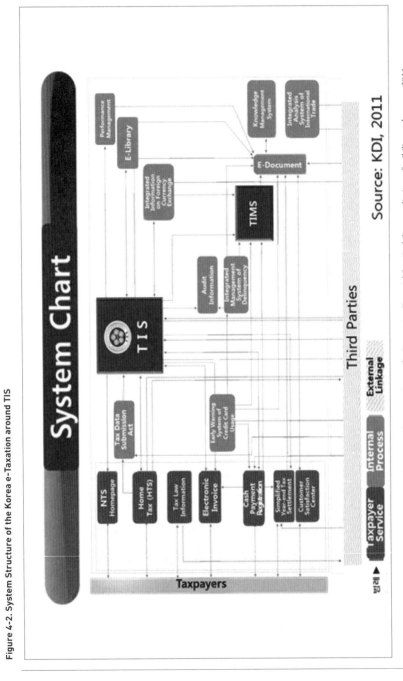

Source: Korea Development Institute, Overhaul of the IRS Information System for Supporting Financial Sustainability, a preliminary feasibility study report, 2011

policies were initiated new systems were attached to the existing system. Table 4-3. summarizes the reasons of adding new systems.

Table 4-3. Reason and status of the individual system

reason	system
Need open system	Knowledge Management, Electronic Document, Cyber Education, Capacity Evaluation, NTS Homepage, Policy Promotion, Law Information System, Advice to National Tax System.
Concern on TIS internal system due to external agencies connection	Foreign Exchange Information System of the Bank of Korea, Defaulter Integrated Management System.
Overloading of TIS due to computation media processing and the bulk of the data processing.	Tax Data Submission and Management System, VAT Tax Base Management System, Early Notification System of Credit Card Transaction.
By need to build up individual security and confidential matters due to the nature of business, System of need to consider that competent department of separate independent operating in the future.	Audit Information System, Internal Audit Management System, Integrated Tax Base Management System.
Separate building in order to minimize the impact of full-service in case of failure and difficult to predict usage due to the nature of service to the public.	Home Tax, Cash Receipt Registration, Simplified Year-End Settlement, EITC, Electronic Invoice.

Building and connecting external systems has caused many problems. System capacities have to be continuously expanded as TIS and other systems has kept duplicating data. Separate systems also resulted in lack of linkage and difficulties in common use of database. A new-generation TIS is now under construction in order to cope with these problems.

4. Employee empowerment

1) Computer and ICT Employees and Organization

(1) Employee

The number of NTS employees in charge of informatization did continuously increase until the introduction of TIS in 1997. Starting from 103 in 1971, it had increased to 1,079 in 1996. This rapid increase occurred mainly for the technical post of data input and processing. As TIS development went on, however, the number of computer specialists increased significantly mainly for system development. After TIS started operating in 1997, technical service employee who mainly worked for data input decreased greatly in number and proportion while the number of computer specialist has increased constantly.

The ratio of employees in the informatization area to the total NTS employees followed a similar pattern. It had increased before the introduction of ITS, but gradually decreased afterwards, reflecting changes in personnel needs in the area of simple and repetitive works, such as data input.

During the TIS development period, the development team that operated consisted of not only computer and informatization experts but also tax officials who had lots of experiences in various taxation areas to ensure the efficiency of the system. In the early days of the TIS operation, the system was jointly operated by system experts from private developers involved in the development and from the NTS. But after a few years of cooperation, the system was operated by only NTS employees. A group of NTS employees, 6 in the system area and 4 in the network area were selected to have external expertise training for 2 years.

Table 4-4. Number and Composition of NTS Employees in Informatization Area

		1971	1990	1996	2000	2009
Personnel (person)	Total NTA (A)	-	16,481	17,838	16,855	19,996
	Total of ICT Employees (B)	185	955	1,079	900	874
	Computer Specialist	82	148	292	294	355
	Tax Official	21	82	65	49	56
	Technical Service	82	725	722	557	463
Proportion (%)	A/B *100		5.79	6.05	5.34	4.37
	Total	100.0	100.0	100.0	100.0	100.0
	Computer Specialist	44.3	15.5	27.1	32.7	40.6
	Tax Official	11.4	8.6	6.0	5.4	6.4
	Technical Service	44.3	75.9	66.9	61.9	53.0

*Source: National Tax Service (each year).

Expertise training of computer and informatization staffs had been commissioned mainly to public institutions such as Korea Institute of Science and Technology (KIST) and the Computer Center at the Ministry of Government Administration, until the mid 1990s, but gradually extended to private and overseas institutions. The curriculum included not only computer-related courses but also those in tax laws and administration, making computer and informatization staff more effective in system development and operation.

But it had been criticized that most of the training program had focused on basic contents and that the training had lacked continuity. IT Expert Management System(EMS), a duty and rank based career development program for computer and informatization staff, was developed in 2005, which has contributed to selecting appropriate personnel in their early career stages and training them.

(2) Organization

The Information System Bureau is responsible for IT and infomatization function in the NTS. The bureau is comprised of 4 departments: System Planning Office, System Operation Office, Information System Development Office 1, and Information System Development Office 2. The System Planning Office is responsible for planning and developing of the system

Figure 4-3. Changes in Informatization Organization

Research Team	Technology Team in Planning and Management Office	Department of Data Processing in Audit Bureau	Office of Data Processing in Bureau of Tax Affairs Management
- 1967.8 - temporary group	- 1968.5 - first permanent organization	- 1969.9 - promoted to department level	- 19870.8 - organizational change

System Operation Office in Collection Bureau	TData Management Bureau and 2 offices	3 offices	2 offices
- 1973.3 - organizational change	- 1974.12 - promoted to bureau level organization	- 1977.3 - Management Office, Data Management Office 1, Data Management Office 2	- 1980.5 - Direct Tax Data Management Office, Indirect Tax Data Management Office

Change in Name	3 Offices	4 Offices	name changes
- 1985.10 - Management Office, Operation Office	- 1990.2 - Management Office, Development Office 1, Development Office 2	- 1994.8 - Management Office, Data Office, Development Office, Business Process Reengineering Office	- 1999.9 - System Planning Office, System Operation Office, System Development Office 1, System Development Office 2

*Source: NTS (2006:358)

and related equipment, and the System Operation Office for management and operation of the equipments and system. And Information System Development Office 1 and Office 2 are responsible for application development and operating related TIS system and HTS systems respectively.

Figure 4-3. shows the changes in the informatization organization in the NTS headquarter office. We can see that the organization has been gradually expanded as the scope and depth of informatization are widened and deepened.

2) General employee empowerment

As computerization and informatization of tax administration went on not only in the information area but in general offices, including provision of PC to all employees by 1997, efforts to enhance computer mind and PCS literacy of the general employees were strengthened. For example, PC ability contests were held and good performers were given various incentives such as additional points on their performance evaluation. Through software contests many excellent programs were selected and applied to actual businesses.

3) Knowledge Management System(KMS)

KMS is the system in which knowledge and experiences of individual members of an organization are systematically classified, stored, and managed, and thereby to be shared and utilized by all members to improve personal and organizational performance. KMS in the NTS which was opened in 2004 with revision to the previous Intranet system has played an important role for employee empowerment. To facilitate the use of the system, incentives such as mileage points were introduced. Major functions

Table 4-5. Major Functions of KMS in NTS

Classification	Functions
Knowledge Plaza	Knowledge Registration, Sharing, Utilization, and Q&A on business related issues
Community	Community of Practice(CoP) activities
Law Information	Search for tax laws and guidelines, etc
Useful Data	Registration of information useful for business, and programs and formats, etc
General Information	Various notification, employee welfare, etc

*Source: NTS (2006:358)

of KMS in the NTS are summarized in Table 4-5.

5. Challenges and solutions

Although the TIS that had taken more than 3 years for development had set the foundation for the Korean e-taxation and had upgraded the level of informatization, a lot of trials and errors had occurred during its initiation period. First at all, too much confidence in the ability of the private developers was placed at the initial stage of the development. A consortium of four private system developers took the responsibility of the system design and construction. They had, however, very scant experience in such a huge system project, thereby were unable to avoid various types of confusion in managing the work flows. For example, there had been significant problems in dividing the work flow and arranging clear responsibility among the developers. The lesson to be learned is that in carrying out such a big informatization project clear definition of work scope and close examination of work environment, such as developers' capacity, need to be carefully prepared in advance.

Moreover, active and voluntary business process reengineering(BPR) led by working organizations was missing. Lack of mutual understanding between IT experts and tax officials had been a recurrent issue in the system development and its operation. Without strong control from the top, taxing departments and bureaus were not in line with the development team. They frequently and persistently resisted informatization of their works in many parts, arguing that manual process was indispensible for many reasons. However, as the chief of development group was not in a position in which he could control taxing departments, it was very difficult to coordinate many related matters such as BPR. Many remedial measures, such as deploying IT experts in tax departments, and offering training sessions for the other area, have been executed. The prime minister's co-chairpersonship of the Presidential Committee on Informatization was a strategy that made e-Government projects more effectively implementable through ministers' active involvement. This experience tells us that to carry out a successful informatization project the project leader must be able to control and coordinate related working organizations.

In case of the HTS introduced in 2002, participation rate in electronic filing was considerably low in the early years. As shown in Table 27., the electronic filing rate of VAT in 2002 was just 17.6%. in 2003, although it increased largely, it still remained low at 33.8%. The government actively responded to the problem in 2004 through the 'Comprehensive Measures to Enhance National Tax Service', one of the 31 primary projects chosen in the e-Government roadmap. In order to promote accession and utilization of the HTS, the NTS mailed Personal Identification Number(PIN) to taxpayers with no accredited certificate to make it easier to join the HTS without visiting the tax office. Tax credit on electronic filing was also introduced. Tax credit of 10,000 Won on electronic filing of VAT, and 20,000 Won on electronic filing of income tax and corporate tax were allowed. To enhance the role of Certified Tax Accountant(CTA), 'Tax Representative Information Integrated Management System' was also introduced to allow CTAs to easily access taxpayers' information. NTS also established the Electronic Filing Task Force for taxing bureaus to review ways of simplification of tax forms and reduction of tax forms to be reported. By developing and incorporating anti-forgery and anti-falsification technology into the system called the 'Internet Civil Services System', taxpayers have been able to issue and print 33 tax-related documents at home, which induced taxpayers to utilize the system more conveniently and frequently.

The TIS, currently constituting the foundation of the Korean e-taxation, began its operation almost 15 years ago. Meanwhile, tax laws and regulations, and other related policies have been frequently revised, and 30 new separate systems have been added and connected to the existing system. For this reason, complexity and duplication of overall systems has been largely increased and a lack of linkage between the systems occured. Accordingly, 'next generation TIS' has been suggested to solve these problems.

6. Conclusion: Implications and Recommendations

The Korean e-taxation has been very successfully carried out.Thereby the level of efficiency in tax administration and the effectiveness of taxpayer services has been greatly enhanced. Such an accomplishment has been indebted to various factors, such as a well equipped infrastructure of high speed broadband networks and social institution, the government's strong policy initiatives and leadership, active participation of taxpayers and NTS officials coupled with various incentives, and a wide variety of services rendered through the system, etc.

Taxpayers and third-parties are other pillars of tax administration. The E-taxation system should be designed user-friendly to secure a higher level of their participation. And an incentive system, such as tax credit for electronic filing could be effective in inducing voluntary participation of taxpayers and tax accountants. Public relations activities should be also actively carried out to improve taxpayers' perception of easiness and convenience of the system.

On the other hand, however, it is also true that there has been much trial-and-error in the process of the informatization of tax administration. At the initial stage of the TIS development there was a lack of coordination among private developers and between taxing departments and the development team. In the case of the HTS the participation rate of taxpayers in electronic filing was quite low initially, and tax officials were quite reluctant to use the new system. As the entire system has become bigger and more complex, many problems such as compatibility and duplication issues have emerged. With the new generation TIS being under construction, taxpayers will be able to get more efficient and more convenient tax administration services.

Human factors seem to be very important for developing a successful e-taxation system, especially in developing countries and at the early stage of system development. Strong leadership and enthusiasm for reform from the top would make it easier to secure sufficient funding and necessary organizational reforms, thereby enable the system to put down its roots firmly. Active involvement of tax officials at the middle and lower levels is also important because they are the people who actually run the system. Training and fostering core tax officials to lead the projects would be a good strategy for this purpose. And it is also important to reduce workloads by curtailing redundant reports which otherwise tend to increase because businesses should be carried out in both ways, that is, in old manual ways and in the new electronic ways, at the initial settling-down stage. The NTS also invested many efforts to have tax officials adapted to the new system through pilot projects, training, and simplification of tax forms, etc. Promoting competition among tax offices and tax officers through a performance evaluation system was another strategy the NTS took.

Tax administration is the process by which tax relations between taxpayers and tax authorities prescribed by tax laws and regulations are actually realized. The key functions of tax authorities are to help taxpayers fulfill their tax duties faithfully and to secure taxpayers compliance through an enforcement process. Even though the informatization of tax administration contributed a lot to these functions, there are still many things to be done. The size of the lowered underground economy estimated to be around 25% needs to be lowed. And there is still much room for the level of satisfaction on the taxpayer services provided by NTS to be enhanced.

Note: This article was funded by and reported to Korea Eximbank in 2012.

References

Korea Development Institute. (2011).*Overhaul of the IRS Information System for Supporting Financial Sustainability*, a preliminary feasibility study report.

Ministry of Strategy and Finance, Korea. (2011).*2011 Korean Taxation*.

National Information Society Agency, NIA. (2012). *Informatization White Paper*.

National Tax Service. (2000).*White Book of the 1999 National Tax Service Reform*.

National Tax Service. (2006).*The 40 Years History of National Tax Service*.

National Tax Service. (each year).*Statistical Yearbook of National Tax*.

Presidential Committee on Government Innovation & Decentralization. (2005).*Public Finance and Taxation Reform of the Participatory Government*.

Presidential Committee on Government Innovation & Decentralization. (2005).*Electronic Government of the Participatory Government*.

Presidential Committee on Government Innovation & Decentralization. (2005). *Serving Government- Field of Innovation and Decentralization*.

Won, Y. (2012).*IT Application in Tax Administration - Korean Experiences*. MIMEO.

Chapter 5

Electronic VAT Invoice System

Hyejung Byun (University of Seoul)

Electronic VAT Invoice System

Hyejung Byun (University of Seoul)

1. Introduction: Why Electronic VAT Invoice System?

1) Why Does VAT Matter?

Taxation provides developing countries with a stable and predictable fiscal environment to promote growth and to finance their social and physical infrastructure. Thus, developing countries try to improve administrative capacity, broaden tax base and increase tax revenue as a proportion of GDP. The United Nations also suggests increasing domestic revenues in low-income countries by around 4 % of GDP.[13] In comparison, most developed

---

13. There are no official definitions of 'developed' or 'developing' countries in the UN system. As World Bank's main criterion, based on the gross national income (hereinafter 'GNI'), every economy is classified as low income, middle income or high income. The middle income economy is subdivided into lower middle and upper middle income. In low income countries, the GNI per capita is $745 or less; in lower middle income counties, $746 - $2,975; in upper middle income countries, $2,976 - $9,205; and in high income countries, $9,206 or more. Country Grouping Glossary, available at http://cyberschoolbus.un.org/infonation3/glossary.html#income (last visited on January 22, 2013)

countries which already have well-developed tax regimes raise, on average, tax revenues equivalent to some 35% of GDP as shown in Table 5-1.

Table 5-1. Total Tax Revenues in OECD Countries

(% of GDP)

	1965	1975	1985	1995	2000	2005	2008	2009	2010
Australia	20.4	25.1	27.5	28.1	30.3	29.8	27.0	25.9	n.a.
Austria	33.9	36.6	40.8	41.4	43.0	42.1	42.8	42.7	42.0
Belgium	31.1	39.5	44.3	43.5	44.7	44.6	44.1	43.2	43.8
Canada	25.7	32.0	32.5	35.6	35.6	33.4	32.2	32.0	31.0
Chile	..	..	..	19.0	19.4	21.6	22.5	18.4	20.9
Czech Republic	..	..	..	37.6	35.2	37.5	36.0	34.7	34.9
Denmark	30.0	38.4	46.1	48.8	49.4	50.8	48.1	48.1	48.2
Estonia	..	..	..	36.3	31.0	30.6	31.7	35.9	34.0
Finland	30.4	36.6	39.8	45.7	47.2	43.9	42.9	42.6	42.1
France	34.2	35.5	42.8	42.9	44.4	44.1	43.5	42.4	42.9
Germany	31.6	34.3	36.1	37.2	37.5	35.0	36.4	37.3	36.3
Greece	17.8	19.4	25.5	28.9	34.0	31.9	31.5	30.0	30.9
Hungary	..	..	..	41.5	39.3	37.3	40.1	39.9	37.6
Iceland	26.2	30.0	28.2	31.2	37.2	40.7	36.7	33.9	36.3
Ireland	24.9	28.7	34.6	32.5	31.2	30.3	29.1	27.8	28.0
Israel	..	..	..	37.0	36.8	35.6	33.8	31.4	32.4
Italy	25.5	25.4	33.6	40.1	42.2	40.8	43.3	43.4	43.0
Japan	18.0	20.7	27.1	26.8	27.0	27.4	28.3	26.9	n.a.
Korea	..	14.9	16.1	20.0	22.6	24.0	26.5	25.5	25.1
Luxembourg	27.7	32.8	39.5	37.1	39.1	37.6	35.5	37.6	36.7
Mexico	..	..	15.5	15.2	16.9	18.1	20.9	17.4	18.7
Netherlands	32.8	40.7	42.4	41.5	39.6	38.4	39.1	38.2	n.a.
New Zealand	23.9	28.4	30.9	36.2	33.1	36.7	33.6	31.5	31.3

Norway	29.6	39.2	42.6	40.9	42.6	43.5	42.9	42.9	42.8
Poland	..	..	..	36.2	32.8	33.0	34.2	31.8	n.a.
Portugal	15.9	19.1	24.5	29.3	30.9	31.2	32.5	30.6	31.3
Slovak Republic	..	..	..	40.3	34.1	31.5	29.4	29.0	28.4
Slovenia	..	..	..	39.0	37.3	38.6	37.0	37.4	37.7
Spain	14.7	18.4	27.6	32.1	34.2	35.7	33.3	30.6	31.7
Sweden	33.3	41.3	47.4	47.5	51.4	48.9	46.4	46.7	45.8
Switzerland	17.5	24.4	25.8	27.7	30.0	29.2	29.1	29.7	29.8
Turkey	10.6	11.9	11.5	16.8	24.2	24.3	24.2	24.6	26.0
United Kingdom	30.4	34.9	37.0	34.0	36.3	35.7	35.7	34.3	35.0
United States	24.7	25.6	25.6	27.8	29.5	27.1	26.3	24.1	24.8
Unweighted average: OECD Total	25.4	29.3	32.5	34.6	35.3	35.0	34.6	33.8	n.a.

*Source: Revenue statistics: Comparative tables, OECD Tax Statistics.

A study shows that developments in tax performance reflect increased revenue from value-added tax (hereinafter 'VAT') as indicated in Figure 5-1. The development requires expanding the tax base by both changing policy and improving compliance rather than increasing standard rates. In developing countries, however, tax policies that might seem very realistic and politically non-controversial are likely to yield a very narrow VAT base. In addition, proper processes have not been established enough to reduce compliance costs and facilitate self-assessment in those countries. Thus, if the government of a developing country wants to rely more on the VAT over time, it needs move aggressively to broaden its base as well as enhance compliance.

Figure 5-1. VAT Revenue in Countries

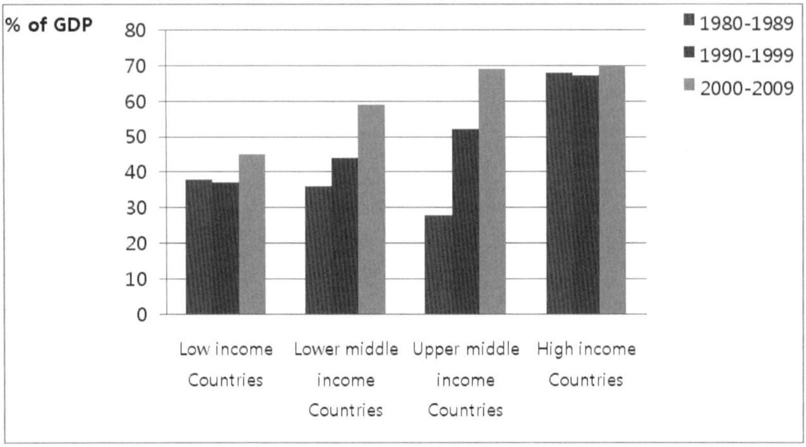

| % of GDP | | | | ■ 1980-1989 ■ 1990-1999 ■ 2000-2009 |

*Source: International Monetary Fund

2) Why Is an Electronic VAT Invoice System Necessary?

The principle of the common VAT system is the invoice-based credit method of the consumption-type VAT. The invoice-based credit method involves the application to goods and services of a general tax on consumption exactly proportional to the prices of the goods and services, whatever the number of transactions takes place in the production and distribution process before the stage at which tax is charged.[14] Thus, the invoice-based credit method requires VAT to be identified in respect of each transaction or group of transactions and issuing VAT invoices in a proper form is an essential part of the procedure for imposing and enforcing VAT. Furthermore, a supplier must issue a VAT invoice to a buyer within certain days

········

14. David Williams (1999), Tax Law Design and Drafting: Value-Added Tax, p. 4, International Monetary Fund. The most important example of another kind of VAT is the accounting method consumption tax adopted in Japan.

from when the goods or services are supplied, which means that there is a strict time limit on issuing VAT invoices. This is so that the buyer can claim back VAT on the supply, if she is entitled to. Consequently, VAT is the most burdensome on business of all taxes for compliance and so an efficient VAT invoicing system is indispensable.

The spread of VAT has been the most important development in taxation over the last half century. Limited to less than ten countries in the late 1960s, VAT has been implemented by more than 150 countries and it accounts for one fifth of the total tax revenue in the OECD and worldwide. Figure 5-2 shows the spread of VAT from the 1980s. As a result of the rapid and widespread adoption of VAT, the systems as well as the laws implementing the tax have adopted different forms in different states. Whatever stage a country stands on now, developing administrative information systems is important to increase the efficiency of VAT collection and reduce compliance costs. Therefore, the aim of this research is to examine the electronic VAT invoice system as an administrative information system required to implement a broad-based VAT and to draw attention to

Figure 5-2. Spread of VAT

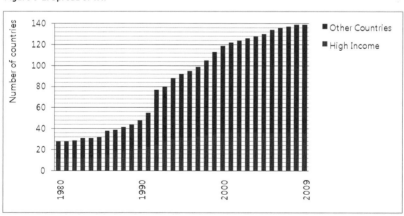

problems requiring solutions for the efficient introduction of the system in developing countries. The example of the Republic of Korea (hereinafter 'Korea') will be referred as a model case.

2. What Is Electronic VAT Invoice?

1) What Is VAT?

Value-Added Tax is a type of consumption tax that is placed on a product whenever value is added at a stage of production and at final sale. The amount of VAT that a buyer pays is the cost of the product, less any of the costs of materials used in the product that have already been taxed. Figure 5-3 shows how VAT operates.

Figure 5-3. Operation of VAT

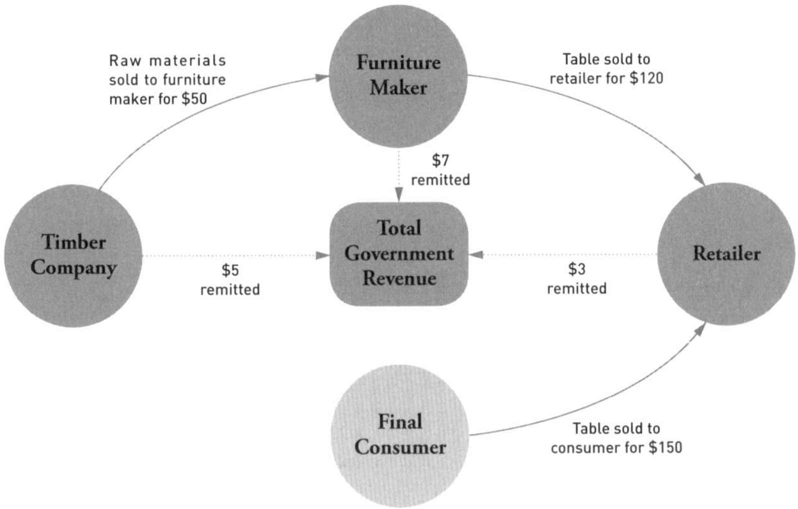

A transaction within the scope of VAT and on which VAT is imposed is commonly called an 'output' and the VAT collected on it is called 'output tax.' A transaction made to a person providing the output is known as an 'input,' and the VAT paid by that person when obtaining the input is an 'input tax.' In Figure 5-3, Timber Company collects $5 of output tax and remits it to the government selling raw materials to Furniture Maker. Furniture Maker collects $12 of output tax, gets $5 of input tax, and remits $7 to the government when it sells the tables to Retailer. Sequentially, Retailer collects $15 of output tax, gets $12 of input tax, and remits $3 of the government selling the table to Final Consumer. The law and system must establish a mechanism that makes the VAT operate properly so that each taxable person is held accountable for the VAT collected on sales and pays the tax over to the tax authorities at regular intervals, after deduction of any allowable input tax.

2) What Is VAT Invoice?

An invoice is a commercial document issued by a supplier to a buyer, indicating the products, quantities, and agreed prices for goods or services that the supplier has provided the buyer. An invoice is a VAT invoice if it complies with the requirement of the VAT law. A VAT invoice should be issued whenever a VAT registered supplier provides goods or services to a buyer who is also registered for VAT.[15] The information of a VAT invoice normally includes:

• the name, address, and VAT registration number of the taxable person

....
15. The registration for the purpose of VAT is to establish a formal state register of those who are registered persons. There are requirements that any person who is, or should be, a taxable person take the necessary action to seek to be registered for VAT.

making the supply,

- the nature of the supply made - type of supply, type of goods or services, and quantity of goods or extent of services,
- the time the supply was made,
- the amount of payment for the supply,
- the amount of VAT,
- the name, address, and VAT number of the taxable person supplied,
- the date on which the invoice is issued, and
- the serial number of the invoice

VAT laws typically condition the allowance of a credit for input tax on the existence of a VAT invoice issued during the period for which the credit is claimed. An invoice is also required by the tax authorities to audit the collection of VAT. To allow these requirements to be met, the law should require a registered supplier making a taxable supply to a registered buyer to provide a VAT invoice with that supply or the payment for it.

3) What Is Electronic VAT Invoicing?

(1) Electronic VAT Invoice

Electronic invoicing is transmission and storage of invoices by electronic means without delivery of paper documents and covers a range of electronic options, including:

- email messages
- document attachments to emails, such as PDF or XML files
- secure networks
- secure websites

- electronic data interchange (EDI)

In this research, electronic VAT invoicing particularly means issuing electronic tax invoices through Internet, ASR/ERP, enterprise accounting system, ARS, or Credit Card Terminal System. Using electronic VAT invoices, business parties can issue, receive and store invoices in electronic format. Thus, if a supplier issues and stores electronic invoices, but fails to meet the requirements, this may mean that the supplier or the buyer does not hold sufficient evidence to reclaim the VAT.

An electronic VAT invoice contains the same information as a paper invoice and as with paper, the supplier needs to keep proper records of the electronic invoice. Thus, as with issuing paper invoices, with an electronic invoice;

- invoice data is complete and accurate
- invoices are sent out when they need to be
- invoices should not be corrupted and should be alerted if problems occur
- duplicate invoices should not accidentally be sent out or should not accidentally be processed twice by buyers, and
- invoices should not automatically be processed and VAT should not be reclaimed when they are not supposed to be.

Table 5-2. Comparison between Paper Invoice and Electronic Invoice

	Paper Invoice	Electronic Invoice
Issue	In paper	In electronic document
Signature	Legal seal	Electronic signature
Receiving	In person or by post	By e-mail
Record Keeping System	Materials base	Computerized record base
Data Search	Manual search	Customized search
VAT Summary Report	Separately filled-in	Automatically transmitted

(2) What Can Be Expected?

The electronic VAT invoice system delivers many benefits to taxpayers and tax authorities. First of all, an electronic VAT invoice decreases reliance on paper and reduces the cost of storage and handling costs. Taxpayers do not have to visit tax offices to obtain authorization to issue new invoices. All parties - senders, recipients and tax authorities have the automated records of the transactions and can access immediately and retrieve easily the record.

VAT systems have been subject to a significant level of fraud and aggressive tax planning over recent years. In VAT systems, tax frauds, avoidance and other abuses can happen by falsifying tax invoices or increasing fake purchases with fake invoices. An electronic VAT invoice makes transactions more transparent and when any disputes are incurred the resolution of disputes can be easier than with a paper invoice because all data is electronically handled and more accurate. Additionally, the electronic invoice facilitates countries exchange of information about various types of abusive practices and prevents cross border tax planning.

(3) Case Study: How Does E-Sero Work in Korea?

In Korea, the use of the electronic VAT invoice system, 'e-sero,' has increased significantly since its launch in 2010. It became compulsory to corporations in 2011 and to self-employed individuals with sales over KRW 1 billion in 2012. As of 2011, 97 percent of taxable persons are using the e-sero to issue invoices. E-sero aims to provide taxpayers with a user-friendly website that allows them to issue invoices carrying the same legal value as paper and offers high standards of information security. Figure 5-4 shows the main feature of e-sero.

Figure 5-4. Main Feature of E-sero

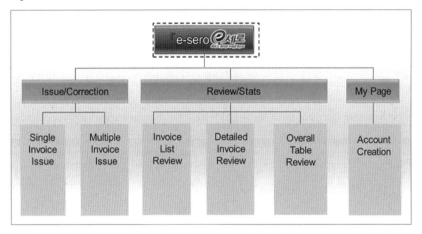

E-sero allows suppliers to issue invoices electronically: suppliers can issue invoices themselves, using their own password, or authorize a third party to issue invoices on their behalf, using their own password. In both cases there is the option of using the data of buyers saved in the system from previous transactions. Suppliers are offered monthly and annual summaries of invoices issued by them or on their behalf. They can download these reports onto their own computers, check on-line all electronic invoices issued, print those invoices and re-send them by e-mail to their recipients. The recipients of electronic invoices are offered monthly reports of all invoices addressed to them. These reports can be used as a record of payments made and taxes withheld to suppliers and can be downloaded onto the taxpayer's computer. The issuers and recipients of electronic invoices are not required to keep the copies of the invoices issued or received electronically or in paper because they can always access them at the website of e-sero.

3. What Conditions are Needed for Establishing Electronic VAT Invoicing?

1) Technical Conditions

The Internet has become a significant tool for the delivery of services to taxpayers and it is a basic requirement to develop electronic tax services. As appeared in Figure 5-5 and Figure 5-6, Korea which successfully launched the

Figure 5-5. Household Internet Access in Korea

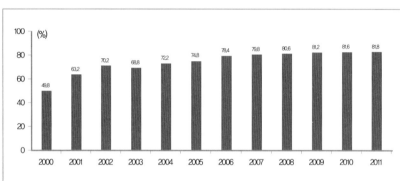

*Source: Won Kim et al, Survey on the Use of the Internet (2011), p. 50, Korea Communications Commission & Korea Internet Security Agency.

Figure 5-6. Household Computer Ownership in Korea

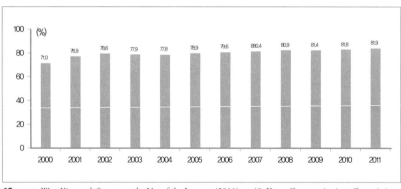

*Source: Won Kim et al, Survey on the Use of the Internet (2011), p. 48, Korea Communications Commission & Korea Internet Security Agency.

electronic tax services including electronic VAT invoice system has high ratios of household internet access and household computer ownership. Table 5-3 shows the top 10 countries of electronic tax services in the world.

Table 5-3. Electronic Tax Service Ranking

Country \ Year	2012	2010	2008	2005	2004	2003	Changes (2001~2010)
Republic of Korea	1	1	6	5	5	13	+12 ↑
Netherlands	2	5	5	12	11	11	+9 ↑
UK and Northern Ireland	3	4	10	4	3	5	+2 ↑
Denmark	4	7	2	2	2	4	=
United States	5	2	4	1	1	1	−4 ↓
France	6	10	9	23	24	19	+13 ↑
Sweden	7	12	1	3	4	2	−5 ↓
Norway	8	6	3	10	10	7	−1 ↓
Finland	9	19	15	9	9	10	+1 ↑
Singapore	10	11	23	7	8	12	+2 ↑

Effective IT systems can reduce compliance costs and facilitate self-assessment. However IT systems in developing countries are often inadequate. Poor results can arise from designing an isolated objective and thus, integrated and complementary systems should be developed. As an example, Table 5-4 shows the development of electronic tax services in Korea.

Electronic tax services' capabilities can be defined within one of four categories of maturity listed in Table 5-5.[16] The phases are generally cumulative and each stage delivers more value to users but also comes with increased complexity and development cost. The electronic VAT invoice system is considered as belonging to the stage of 'Integration'. Thus, a devel-

Table 5-4. Development of Electronic Tax Services in Korea

YEAR	SYSTEM	KEY FUNCTIONS
1997	Tax Integrated System	Key systems for NTS officials
1999	NTS Homepage	Information and guidance about NTS
2000	Electronic Document System	Producing and keeping digitized official documents
2002	Hometax	Tax return, tax payment, civil petition and notification
2003	Tax Information Management system	Statistics and analysis
2004	Knowledge Management System	Creation and sharing of information among NTS officials
2005	Cash Receipt System	Collecting and managing cash receipt data from all transactions
2006	Simplified Year-end Tax Settlement	Providing year-end tax adjustment data to wage earners
2006	National Tax Law Information System	Providing tax legislation
2010	Electronic VAT Invoice System	Transmitting and storing VAT invoice

Table 5-5. Electronic Tax Service Maturity

Category	Description	Confidentiality
		Access
Presence (Information)	One way information flow providing static information about the agency. Includes publications (e.g. legislation, policy documents), instructions, and education/ marketing materials. Interaction is limited to inquiry & search functions.	Publicly available/ non-confidential data
		No access restrictions

• • • • • • • •

16. In general, electronic tax services cover all electronic interactions and include: tax information via the Internet; electronic filing of tax returns; pre-filed tax returns; electronic payments; access to personal taxpayer information via online taxpayer accounts; and call centres. As to the call centres, while traditional phone services (e.g. person-to-person call centres) are not generally defined as 'e-services', they have been included here as the survey (based on this framework) examined the full range of service offerings provided by revenue bodies via phone services. Centre for Tax Policy and Administration (2010), Survey of Trends and Developments in the Use of Electronic Services for Taxpayer Service Delivery, p. 9, OECD.

Interaction	Two-way information flow which does not alter systems or data. This includes expanded search and filtering capabilities and services such as calculators where all data are entered by users (e.g. to assess eligibility for benefits or determine tax payable).	Publicly available/ non-confidential data
		No access restrictions
Transaction	Any exchange which alters data holdings or provides access to taxpayer data. Includes activities such as enquiries involving taxpayer data, use of calculators pre-filed with taxpayer data, & filing returns/ making payments.	Confidential data
		Access restricted to specific individual
Integration (Transformation)	Exchange of information between different government agencies regarding a specific user (individual, business, organisation). For example, a change of address advised only once by the user and then shared across relevant agencies.	Confidential data
		Access restricted to specific individual

*Source: Centre for Tax Policy and Administration (2010), Survey of Trends and Deployments in the Use of Electronic Services for Taxpayer Service Delivery, OECD.

oping country adopting the system should have to go through all the previous stages of 'Presence', 'Interaction' and 'Transaction'.

2) Systemic Conditions

In general, when certain electronic tax services including electronic invoicing, electronic filing and electronic payment are mandatorily required of taxpayers, significant benefits and costs savings can accrue to both tax authorities and taxpayers. Korea introduced mandated requirements for corporations and self-employed individuals that supply the goods or services of KRW 1 billion or over and plans to extend the use of those requirements to some smaller or all business operators. Appropriate penalties are necessary to set up and operate the system properly. Table 5-6 describes the penalties imposed on each violation in Korea. At the same time, Korea also adopted an incentive rule, under which taxpayers can get tax credit of KRW 200 per invoice and its annual limit is KRW 1,000,000.

Table 5-6. Penalties on Violation of Electronic VAT Invoicing Rules in Korea

	Issuer	Recipient
No Issue	2%	Input tax is not deducted
Late Issue	1%	1%
No Transmission	0.3%	N/A
Late Transmission	0.1%	N/A

However, there is a risk in pursuing a policy of mandating the use of electronic tax services on any significant scale where these services are not already well entrenched. Mandating the use of poorly-designed services is likely to lead to additional administrative burden. Complaints and dissatisfaction with the services may arise and also result in a broader degree of reluctance to use other services which will be offered by the tax authority in the future. Thus, as mentioned earlier, technical infrastructure and condition should be developed enough to adopt electronic tax services.

4. What Are Competencies Necessary for Tax Officials and Employees?

1) Good Tax Administration

A tax system is as good as its tax administration and without improvement in these administrations, it is unlikely that developing countries mobilize domestic financial resources for development. In most developing countries, it may be required creating an independent revenue service which is free from corruption and political interference.

2) Employees with Expertise

Increasing the range of electronic tax services including electronic VAT invoicing is an important strategy to improve taxpayer service delivery. In order to enable electronic tax services to be successfully launched and fully utilized by taxpayers, tax authorities should have the ability to operate the systems properly and effectively and need experts in computer, data processing and other technical matters. In Korea, for example, IT staff account for 4.3 percent of all NTS personnel: among 19,996 NTS personnel, 200 IT staff are assigned to the head office, 246 to 6 regional offices and 411 to 107 district offices. They are composed of 333 (38%) computer experts, 467 (56%) technicians and 57 (6%) administrations.

3) Collaboration

The goal of an overall strategy for work on electronic tax services is to ensure coordinated services, reduce paperwork and achieve a development. To effectively establish the electronic VAT invoice system, a public sector should be cohesive, better co-ordinated and capable of building and providing the services expected. Furthermore, a public sector must be more open and make a targeted effort to involve citizens and businesses in the development of digital solutions to pursue a more collaborative relationship. Close collaboration is also required between the public sector, software producers, and agents, supported by a program targeted at potential users to explain the benefits of the service and computerisation in general.

4) Security and Privacy

Tax authorities should make efforts to guarantee the safe and secure handling of data that they acquire. They must become more technologically sophisticated to meet increased taxpayer expectations and maintain data security, by modernizing the systems, improving their employee training program, and continually enhancing the safeguards.

5. Challenges & Solutions

1) How to Optimize the Electronic VAT Invoice System?

(1) Accessibility

It is clear that to achieve very high rates of electronic tax service take-up, all potential users including those not in possession of their own equipment must have access to the Internet and be able to easily find what they are seeking as well as use specific applications. However citizens in rural and remote locations are less likely to know how to contact tax offices online while those over age 65 are most likely to find the website too hard to use. As a strategy to increase accessibility, it should be considered providing new service outlets including through use of community libraries, workplaces, government shopfront facilities, kiosks, and private sector organizations, both for general convenience as well as for those citizens who do not have their own personal computers. Furthermore, given the increasing international transaction and non-resident taxpayers, the provision of public electronic services needs to follow standards and international guidelines for accessibility.[17]

(2) Ease of Use

Electronic tax services should be convenient and should not be complicated to use. Many taxpayers feel comfortable with paper form built up over many years and a new system would require a lot more effort, if it is not easy enough to use. Thus, adopting any new system, there is a concern that the new system would require a significant effort to adjust to without offering substantial advantages. In addition, if there are additional costs involved, the new system will fail in enhancing tax compliance. Another concern is that negative experiences with a specific electronic service would discourage the use of other services in the future.

Taxpayers who have never used electronic tax services may find it hard to imagine how the process would work in practice and how similar it would be to the paper forms they felt familiar with. Even those who are relatively optimistic about using electronic tax services may not be easily diverted from making paper invoicing to using the electronic one. In these cases, taxpayers would feel the actual process of registering for the service, waiting for a PIN and becoming familiar with the site is too much effort and anxiety on top of deadlines. As a solution of this issue, the capabilities of online customer services and call centers should be stimulated to help taxpayers.

Another solution is making the electronic form as similar to the paper form as possible, by using similar language and design regarding each item and section. It would provide reassurance and help build confidence, especially among those that were less confident regarding IT and interact less regularly with the website providing the electronic VAT invoice system.

· · · · · · · ·
17. For example, official websites must adhere to the international Web Accessibility Initiative (WAI) guidelines.

(3) Personalization

While taxpayers desire that the electronic form have the same look and feel as the paper version intended to be replaced, they also expect that the use of the electronic form leads to some tangible benefits for users. Thus, a new electronic tax service should be sufficiently personalized or differentiated to make taxpayers feel convenience in using the new service and reduce taxpayers' compliance burden. The new system needs to be tailored to user's needs and lessen questions asking about each person's circumstances by automatically presenting information which tax authorities already hold. In addition, it can be expected that electronic services enable taxpayers or their representatives to express their preferences for the range and nature of the specific electronic services to be provided to them and how that will be managed.

2) How to Increase Security and Protect Privacy?

As more people gain access to the Internet and as IT systems become more inter-connected, data security concerns rise. Many taxpayers are concerned that electronic VAT invoicing may not be fully reliable or secure. Thus, appropriate security and privacy protection safeguards have been recognized as critical. The security measures in place to protect taxpayers' personal information are stringently in line with those used by other organizations which promote electronic transactions such as financial institutions. In Korea, as security measures, network encryption, digital signaturing and PC firewalls are concurrently used for the electronic VAT invoice system.

6. Conclusion: Recommendation and Implication

Governments restructure their tax systems to achieve their social and economic objectives and, at the same time, secure the revenue required to finance their expenditure. Adopting innovative tax services, they should identify that they can promote greater voluntary compliance and reduce costs for taxpayers with these services.

When the government of a developing country wants to rely more on the VAT over time, it must move aggressively to broaden the tax base and enhance compliance. Such policies may require harder political choices than is usually required from governments of most industrialized countries. Resources should be spent to enhance the effectiveness of the tax administration. The present policy maker determines the efficiency of the tax system of the next period.

The electronic VAT invoicing is an important measure to enhance taxpayer's convenience and decrease costs. Furthermore, it can prevent abuses by falsifying tax invoices or increasing fake purchases with fake invoices. To successfully establish the electronic VAT invoice method, basically, taxpayers should be able to access the Internet and use the electronic VAT invoice website. The system should be convenient and should not be complicated to use. In addition, it should be sufficiently personalized or differentiated to make taxpayers feel that it is convenient to use the new service and reduce the taxpayers' compliance burden. The security and privacy protection also becomes a critical issue to develop the electronic service, and security measures including network encryption, digital signature and PC firewall should be included in the system.

Note: This article was funded by and reported to Korea Eximbank in 2012.

References

Centre for Tax Policy and Administration. (2008).*Programs to Reduce the Administrative Burden of Tax Regulations*. OECD.

Centre for Tax Policy and Administration. (2009).*Developments in VAT Compliance Management in Selected Countries*. OECD.

Centre for Tax Policy and Administration. (2010).Programs to Reduce the Administrative Burden of Tax Regulations (Follow-up Report). OECD.

Centre for Tax Policy and Administration. (2010).*Survey of Trends and Developments in the Use of Electronic Services for Taxpayer Service Delivery*. OECD.

Centre for Tax Policy and Administration. (2011).*Forum on Tax Administration: Tax Administration in OECD and Selected Non-OECD Countries: Comparative Information Series (2010)*. OECD.

Centre for Tax Policy and Administration. (2012).*Working smarter in revenue administration - Using demand management strategies to meet service delivery goals*. OECD.

Fiscal Affairs Department. (2011).*Revenue Mobilization in Developing Countries, International Monetary Fund*.

Jenkins, Glenn P. and Kuo, Chun-Yan. (2000). A VAT Revenue Simulation Model for Tax Reform in Developing Countries.*World Development*, 28(4):763-774.

National Tax Service. (2011).*E-Service in Korea*. National Tax Service.

Kim, Won et al. (2011).*Survey on the Use of the Internet*. Korea Communications Commission & Korea Internet Security Agency.

http://www.esero.go.kr/

Chapter 6

Searching for a Seamless E-Government Solution for Social Welfare Administrations: Korea's Social Welfare Integrated Management Network (SWIMN)

M. Jae Moon (Yonsei University)

Searching for a Seamless E-Government Solution for Social Welfare Administrations: Korea's Social Welfare Integrated Management Network (SWIMN)*

M. Jae Moon (Yonsei University)

1. Introduction

Social welfare programs have been experiencing expansion in many countries as a result of increasing attention to quality of life and social protection issues. Many governments often expand existing social protection programs or initiate new social welfare programs for the disadvantaged and vulnerable population in their societies. Social welfare programs are, in fact, almost always a part of key policy interests for central and local governments.

Recently, many Asian-Pacific countries have also begun to pay more interest to social development and social security programs that extend beyond economic development to include substantial responses to social demand for a good quality of life. With the expansion of social security

....
* This chapter is written largely based on the government information on the Social Welfare Integrated Management Network.

programs, as Asian countries begin to expand and improve their social welfare programs, they also face multiple challenges with a rapidly increasing volume of social welfare service-related data (residence, income, property, taxes, and other related information) as well as a lack of effectiveness and transparency in social security administration. In fact, these challenges are not new ones. Developed countries have already experienced similar problems and often responded by actively implementing technological solutions to enhance efficiency, effectiveness, and transparency in social security administration.

Technological solutions often take the form of e-Government projects. There are two main dimensions of e-Government for social welfare administration: 1) back-office applications and 2) front-office applications. Back-office applications refer to the applications of information and communication technology (ICT) for the internal management of data and cases, as well as internal decision-making processes. Internal management of data includes the creation, storage, processing, and analysis of the digitized data. Internal decision-making refers to social welfare program-related internal administration. Front-office applications of ICTs often refer to the establishment of ICT systems for electronic service provisions of various social welfare benefits to beneficiaries. The electronic service system often covers a multi-step process, from applications to a particular social welfare program to the provision of services to a target population.

In particular, many developing countries have become more interested in ICT-based social welfare administration as they strive to design a more efficient, effective, accountable and transparent system for social security administration; their strategy has included applying ICT to both back-office and front-office applications. Governments need to process and manage more than just an increasing amount of social welfare-related personal information. They must also integrate multiple pieces of individual information (demographics, property, taxes, financial information, etc.) as well as different social welfare services, which are often managed by different public agencies and different levels of governments.

Governments tend to implement e-Government projects with the goal of attaining an integrated and seamless information management system that will transform and improve their social welfare administration. Of course, this transformation of the system is not an easy task. It often requires an adequate planning capacity, interagency collaboration, financial resources, citizen involvement, infrastructure, etc. This study is designed to review the development of the Social Welfare Integrated Management Network (SWIMN), established in 2010 by the Korean government, to improve the efficiency and effectiveness of its social welfare administration. SWIMN's main targets are to successfully integrate central government and local government systems as well as to integrate the existing information and service systems of multiple public agencies. We will review the emerging significance of the e-Government approach to social welfare administration. Then, a case study of SWIMN will be presented by surveying its legal, institutional, organizational, and technical background. The human resources development issue will be also discussed. Finally, some managerial and technical lessons will be drawn for those who will be planning similar systems in the future.

2. Growing Social Welfare Programs in Asia and the E-Government Approach

Social security programs often include allowances for families for the support of their children. The programs also provide financial assistance to compensate for at least a portion of income lost due to a multitude of both predicted and unpredicted causes: old age, disability, death, illness, maternity leave, work injury, unemployment, hospitalization, medical care, and rehabilitation (Social Security Administration, 2010). The programs take the form of cash payments and/or benefits-in-kind. Major social security programs include the national pension system, the public health insurance system, and various social welfare programs for various disadvantaged target groups, such as the low income and handicapped populations and survivor populations, such as widows and their children. Social welfare programs are often categorized into the following five distinct groups: old age, disability, and survivors; sickness and maternity; work injury; unemployment; and family allowances. Each group includes various programs as identified in the following Table6-1.:

Table 6-1. Types of Social Security Programs

Category	Primary Program	Financial Sources	Administering Agency
Old age, disability, and survivors	Pension / Survivor benefits / Disability benefits	-Employee contribution- Employer contribution -Government contribution	Semiautonomous institutions or funds
Sickness and maternity	Healthcare/ Medical insurance	-Employee contribution -Employer contribution	Semiautonomous institutions or funds
Work injury	Cash benefits or medical care for work injuries	-Employer contribution	Semiautonomous institutions or funds -Private carriers
Unemployment	Weekly pay benefit for the unemployed	Employer contribution -Government subsidies	Government departments or self-governing institutions
Family allowances	Children allowances	General fund of the government	Government departments

*Source: Compiled from SSA and ISSA (2012).

Social welfare programs in Asia are experiencing dramatic expansion as

Asian economies continue to advance and begin paying more attention to achieving a balance between economic development and social development. Despite the increasing attention and interest in social security programs, Asia and the Pacific region are still far behind the global average in terms of public expenditure on their public social security. For example, public social security expenditure as a percentage of GDP in the Asian and the Pacific region is 6.9%, while the global average is 10.9%. Western European countries spend about 23.2% of GDP on public social security; even Latin American and Caribbean countries spend about 7.4% of GDP as the following figure indicates:

Figure 6-1. Total Social Protection in Percentage of GDP by Region

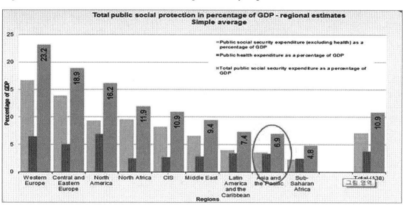

Source: ILO (2010).

This graph shows that the proportion of public security expenditure as a percentage of GDP in the Asian and Pacific region is far less than in most other regions in the world. In fact, every region, except the Sub-Saharan African region, allocates a greater proportion of its GDP to public security programs than the Asian and Pacific region. Asian and Pacific countries need to pay more attention to social security programs for the welfare of their populations. A wide gap in social security has also been reported within Asian and Pacific countries (Baulch et.al. 2008). For example, the social security index for Pakistan is 0.07, which is much lower than the regional average (0.36); on the other hand, that of India (0.46) and China (0.45) are a little above the regional average.

While the performance of social security programs in the Asian-Pacific region is somewhat behind the world average, e-Government performance in the region is a bit higher than the world average. The United Nations' e-Government index confirms this finding. There is a wide variation, however, in the development of e-Government systems within the Asian-Pacific region. For example, the performance of e-Government systems in Eastern Asia is far better than the global average; however, Southern Asia is far behind the rest of the world in this respect. The other sub-regions such as Central, Southeast, and Western Asian regions are more or less close to the

Figure 6-2. E-Government Performance by Region

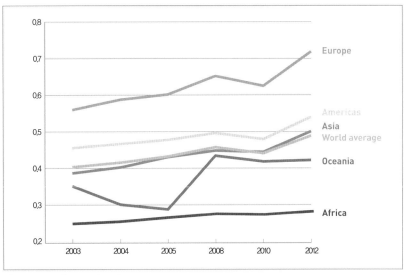

*Source: United Nations (2012).

global average of e-Government performance. Figure 6-2 shows the variation in the e-Government performance of various sub-regions in the Asian-Pacific region:

It has been widely recognized that the development gap among countries can be technologically addressed and solved by governments' proactive applications of ICTs. In fact, ICTs have offered new opportunities for underdeveloped countries to improve the capacity of their administrative mechanisms as well as the quality of the delivery of their services. ICTs have been recognized to be an excellent tool which enhances the performance level of the social welfare administration as well as the quality of social welfare programs and services.

When promoting social welfare programs, many countries have been faced with various administrative challenges at various stages of service delivery. These challenges have included the determination of eligibility in each case, the management of beneficiary databases, the documentation of each case, the administration of payments or service delivery to beneficiaries, feedback and monitoring, and the integration of various social welfare programs. These challenges could be effectively addressed and solved by various ICT solutions.

3. Overview and Basic Structure of SWIMN

SWIMN is an integrated ICT-based social welfare management system which seamlessly connects various databases of social welfare benefits, qualification data, and the employment history of recipients of social welfare; this conglomeration of databases supports social service delivery by local governments as well as enhances the efficiency and transparency of the social welfare administration. The need for an integrated system began to be identified by people who criticized the past welfare service system by claiming that it wasn't responding effectively to the rapid increase in the number of social welfare beneficiaries, the diversification of the welfare environment, the growing demand for customized services, and serious concerns about the possibility of fraud and the abuse of social welfare benefits.

Despite the continued average increase in the annual social welfare budget of 12.2%, the social service delivery system was not appropriately developed. Because of the increasing budget, the growing number of beneficiaries, and the complex selection procedure, local governments suffered from an unprecedentedly heavy workload. With the increasing case workload and program expansion, and the great need for integrated systems for efficient social welfare administration, social welfare agencies faced great pressure to develop an effective standardization of selection criteria and procedures for different social welfare programs. At the same time, beneficiaries were also becoming increasingly dissatisfied because they were required to apply and receive counsel for each program separately. Social welfare services were managed as provider-oriented programs and not as customer-oriented programs. According to a satisfaction survey, about 65% of social welfare beneficiaries responded that they were not satisfied with the system. There was also a growing concern about inefficiency of welfare financing because of an increasing number of fraud cases and occurrences of double payments. The government also began to experience difficulties in identifying potential beneficiaries who were not eligible but in need of public assistance; this difficulty occurred because social welfare public officials were so occupied by their routine administrative work (MHWS, 2011).

Responding to these problems in its social welfare service system, the Korean government decided to develop an integrated social welfare service network. It did this by establishing integrated social welfare information systems which aimed at unifying information channels by integrating social service delivery systems handled by different institutions such as the central government, local governments, and private actors. This project was selected as one of 36 core projects of the Lee Myung-bak administration (MHWS, 2011).

Figure 6-3. Paradigm Shift from the Sae-all Administration System to SWIMN

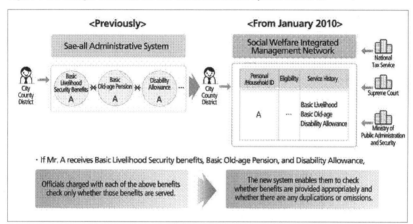

The system basically separates social welfare information from the existing Sae-all Administration System of local governments and then integrates it into the new integrated system where 31 types of individual information (resident, land, finance, taxes, welfare, etc.) are comprehensively integrated. SWIMN mainly aims to prevent inaccuracies and omissions in social benefit payments, promote transparency in welfare administration, provide more practical welfare benefits, and reduce the administrative burden. SWIMN is also designed to ensure the integrated management of databases at the individual and household level by establishing benefit history databases of both individuals and households. It also attempts to standard-ize and simplify the procedures for recipient selection as well as to provide user-friendly customized needs for welfare. SWIMN also promotes trans-parent payment of various welfare benefits by computerizing and system-izing the benefit payment procedures.

In order to make the social welfare service system simpler, more custom-er-oriented, more efficient, more accountable, and more effective, SWIMN was equipped with the following features (KHWIS homepage)[18] :

- Providing a one-stop application by identifying the needs of the appli-cant and designing the necessary services without any omissions.
- Increasing user convenience by integrating similar or overlapped forms and replacing the necessary documents with public data; this reduced the 37 previously-required documents to 6 documents.
- Providing welfare benefits and services more quickly by shortening the period of processing and notification of the applicant of the results from letters sent through the mail to SMS (short message service) or e-mail.
- Informing the recipient of additional services to prevent the omission of any benefit; highlighting the availability of additional support in such cases as age change and change in physical conditions which af-fect eligibility and benefit amount.
- Providing services by connecting with the Health & Welfare Call Cen-ter and call centers in each district.
- Improving accuracy in selecting the recipients of social welfare services and paying appropriate benefits by connecting 213 data items includ-ing income, assets, personal information, and service history in a num-ber of institutions. Additionally, integrating and managing the data of

18. KHWIS homepage (http://www.khwis.or.kr/eng/main.do)

120 welfare benefits and the service histories of individuals and households to prevent duplicate payments (excerpted from KHWIS homepage: http://www.kKHWIS.or.kr/eng/pageFwr.do?sd=PS&ms=711).

The major structure and core elements of SWIMN are summarized in Figure 6-4. The figure highlights the procedure of how an individual social welfare application is processed and integrated into other social service programs, and then how different databases and institutions are interconnected to form an integrated social welfare administration.

Figure 6-4. The Main Structure of SWIMN

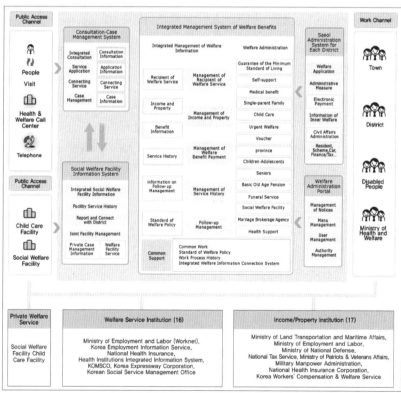

*Source: http://www.kKHWIS.or.kr/eng/pageFwr.do?sd=PS&ms=711

To incorporate these features into the system, SWIMN integrates private welfare service providers, 16 welfare service institutions, and 17 income and property-related institutions as shown in the figure. Different types of welfare-related information are integrated seamlessly so that the basic tasks of selecting beneficiaries, screening eligibility, and the automation of the welfare systems are efficiently managed. This enables the government to prevent fraud, abuse, and double payments of social welfare benefits. According to estimates calculated by the Korean government, SWIMN saved about KRW 247 billion in 2010 from 6 different social welfare programs (see Table 6-2). In fact, the estimated savings is more than what the government spent (KRW 10.7 billion) for SWIMN in the same year. SWIMN also reduced the administrative time, from 60 days to 14 days, to process applications and complete all the necessary steps leading to a final section decision.[19]

Table 6-2. Savings from Preventing Frauds and Incorrect Payments

(Unit: KRW Million)

Item	Savings by Preventing Frauds and Double Payments of Benefits		
	2009	2010	Total
Basic Life Security	80,773	247,990	171,220
Basic Elderly Pension	50,970	120,250	25,506
Childcare Assistance	8,070	17,436	113,334
Single Parent Assistance	17,294	96,040	8,527
Disabilities Assistance	1,726	6,801	8,365
Disabilities Pension	2,713	5,652	1,811
Total	80,773	247,990	328,763

*Source: MHWS (2011:131)

• • • • • • • •
19. http://www.ciociso.com/news/articleView.html?idxno=9538

4. Legal and Institutional Background of SWIMN[20]

The development of a particular e-Government solution, such as SWIMN, does not take place in a sudden way. Many factors are prerequisite for the successful planning, development, execution, and utilization of a particular e-Government system. The determining factors include the legal and institutional framework, the ICT infrastructure, the government's vision and capacity for information strategy planning (ISP), its implementation capacity, its financial resources, the users' ICT skills, political support for the system, etc. Since the 1970s, the Korean government has pursued the computerization of public administration when it initiated the Basic Planning for Computerization of Public Administration. This initiative was then greatly enhanced by the Basic Planning for the Promotion of National Informatization of 1995 then further advanced by the Framework Act of National Informatization of 2010 (Jung, 2011). While national informatization was pursued by the Korean government for a long period of time, the comprehensive informatization initiatives in the social welfare area are a relatively recent phenomenon. The Korean government began to pay more attention to the informatization of social welfare administration (the social welfare information service system) beginning in the mid-1990s though the digitization of social welfare administration data. This achievement, starting with early computerization initiatives for public administration, was the culmination of work carried out by the Korean government over a long time period.

In particular, the digitization of social welfare data became a great foundation for the comprehensive social welfare information systems. The Na-

---

20. Some part of this section is based on information obtained from MOPAS (2011) and MHWS (2011). For additional information on the Korean e-government and SWIMN, see MOPAS (2011) and MHWS (2011), respectively.

tional Database Computerization Project (MOPAS 2011) was implemented between 1987 and 1996. This project basically aimed to establish digitized national databases for key areas including administration, finance, education, research, and defence. The project was pursued at two different stages. The government spent KRW 2,470 billion, in the first stage (1987-1991); at this point, it digitized basic personal information, including resident registration, real estate registration, etc. In the second stage using KRW 4,450 billion, the government then established digitized databases for public welfare, economy, trade, and other areas. It is important that the Korean government pursued the National Database Computerization Program with a so-called "settlement after investment" scheme which allowed private developers to develop the digitized databases and then have their expenses reimbursed later by the government.

Based on the digitized social welfare database, the government attempted to develop the social welfare information service system to enhance the effectiveness, efficiency, productivity, and transparency of the social welfare administration where many public agencies at different levels of government and stakeholders such as citizens, social service providers, and private actors are involved. The social welfare information system was introduced as part of an aggressive e-Government initiative which began in the 2000s after the Comprehensive Plan for Construction of Korean Information Infrastructure of 1995. The Korean government strategically selected 31 key e-Government projects in four different areas, which established a strong foundation for integrated e-Government systems (including the Social Welfare Integrated Management Network).

Continuing to pursue its overall objectives, the Korean government has recently made efforts to promote seamless and integrated e-Government systems that connect and integrate different databases and service systems.

Table 6-3. Key E-Government Project in the Early 2000s

Area	Project
Innovating the Way Government Works	11 Projects – digitalizing the entire document processing procedure, realizing local e-Government, and real-time management of national agenda
Innovating Public Service	14 Projects – improving Internet-based civil services, single-window for business support services, and increasing online citizen participation
Innovating Information Resource Management	5 Projects – building Government Integrated Data Center (GIDC), building information security system, and stepping up informatization organizations and personnel
Innovating Legal Systems	Reforming laws and regulations for –Government and security

*Source: MOPAS (2011:19)

With continued efforts towards the integration of databases and service systems, the number of information resources was recently reduced from 4,687 in 2008 to 2,535 in 2010 (MOPAS, 2011). The integration of different databases and systems has allowed the government to manage information resources more efficiently.

During the Korean presidential election in December, 2007, the President pledged to establish an efficient welfare delivery system by integrating the welfare information held by central, local, and private systems as well as to unify its information channels. To actualize this presidential pledge, the government developed the basic framework for SWIMN in April, 2008 and also made specific plans for basic business process reengineering (BPR) and Information Strategy Planning (ISP) in December 2008 (MHWS 2011). Along with the revision of the Social Welfare Services Act in 2009, the government officially completed SWIMN in 2010. The government also developed additional functions for SWIMN to ensure the security of the system.

With the revision of the Social Welfare Services Act in 2009, the Korean government paved the road for the construction of the Social Welfare Integrated Management Network. According to the Social Welfare Services Act, central and local governments are responsible for developing SWIMN to allow the public and private sectors to share social welfare information in order to prevent any illegal payments (fraud and abuse) of social benefits. The law also stipulated specific penalties that would be imposed on those who misused private information in the course of operating the Social Welfare Integrated Management Network. In order to establish and operate the Social Welfare Integrated Management Network, the Korean government established the Korean Health and Welfare Information Service (KHWIS) under the supervision of the Ministry of Health and Welfare Services. KHWIS was established as an agency whose function was limited to the social welfare system; however, it was later expanded to handle public health services because public health services are administered by the Ministry of Health and Welfare Services.

5. Organizational Background: Inter-agency Coordination and the Establishment of KKHWIS[21]

1) Inter-agency Tension and Inter-agency Coordination

When the Social Welfare Integrated Management Network was built, there was disagreement among related agencies, particularly between the Ministry of Public Administration and Security (MOPAS) and the Ministry of Health and Welfare Services (MHWS). MOPAS contended that the system should be connected to the existing Sae-all Public Administration System,

••••••••
21. This is based on information acquired from the White Paper published by MHWS's (2011).*White Paper on the Integrated Social Welfare Information System*

which is a basic public administration information system for local governments. MOPAS wanted to manage the Social Welfare Integrated Management Network because the Sae-all Administration System was established and managed by MOPAS. Emphasizing the fact that MOPAS had already established the Sae-all Administration System for local governments in 2007, MOPAS strongly argued that SWIMN might possibly infringe on the autonomy of local governments if the beneficiaries of social welfare services were selected by the central government.

However, MHWS presented a different opinion which argued that the Integrated Social Welfare System should be managed by MHWS for the sake of efficiency and operational fit with the function of the ministry. This disagreement became a serious impediment to the SWIMN project because the positions of the two ministries were irreconcilable. Though the tension between MOPAS and MHWS was the most compelling and visible conflict, there were many other agencies which expressed some concern about sharing the information that they held because the new integrated system involved extensive sharing of public information, such as tax information, income information, property, international travel information, etc. Reaching an agreement to share the information managed by different agencies was a challenging task. This process actually caused unexpected tension among related agencies, including the Supreme Court, Korean Tax Services (KTS), the Korea Pension Service (KPS), the National Health Insurance Service (NHIS), the Korea Employment Information Service (KEIS), the Korea Youth Counseling and Welfare Institute (KYCI), etc.

To resolve these interagency conflicts, the Prime Minister's Office convened meetings to settle the problem. It made efforts to play a significant role in coordinating participating agencies and reaching an agreement among them. Particularly, the conflict between MOPAS and MHWS received serious attention, but was not resolved easily. Eventually, a policy position was established that made MHWS responsible for SWIMN, so that the Social Welfare component of the Sae-all Administration System of Local governments was to be incorporated into SWIMN.

Once the decision was made, SWIMN required the reorganization of local governments. To effectively structure SWIMN, the division of labour between the different levels of governments was clarified. Two alternative positions were under discussion. The first alternative was that the city, county, and district (Si, Gun, and Gu) levels of local governments would take the responsibility of selecting beneficiaries by conducting wealth and income investigations and then the sub-levels of local governments (Dong) would be in charge of counsel, case management, and searching for unidentified potential beneficiaries. The second alternative was to make the sub-levels of governments (Dong) responsible for case selection, decision of benefits, and payment, and then the city, county, and district (Si, Gun, and Gu) levels of local governments would be responsible for identifying unidentified potential beneficiaries experiencing unexpected difficulties. After long debates on this matter, the first alternative was finally adopted; the city, county, and district levels of local governments would establish integrated investigation and management teams for social welfare services based on income, property, and related information collected by the sub-levels (Dong) of governments. The system basically integrated more than 50 different types of public information, as well 219 different kinds of social service related information managed by 27 public institutions. Figure 6-5. shows some examples of public information and institutions that are integrated into SWIMN. For the long term, the Korean government also even considered a possible future linkage between SWIMN and private sector resources in order to extend integration beyond the public sector (MHWS, 2011).

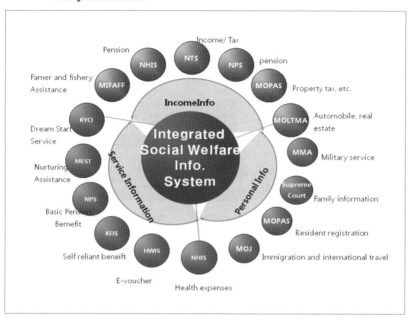

*Source: MHWS (2011).

2) The Establishment of the Korea Health and Welfare Information Service (KHWIS)

After the Korean government reached the position that SWIMN would be basically managed by MHWS, it established the Korea Health and Welfare Information Service (KKHWIS) in December 2009 to be the administrative and operating body in charge of project implementation in order to effectively construct and manage SWIMN. KHWIS essentially functions as a central control which is in charge of the establishment and operation of management information systems in the area of social welfare and health services under the supervision of the Ministry of Health and Welfare Service.

Figure 6-6. Mission, Vision, and Core Values of KHWIS

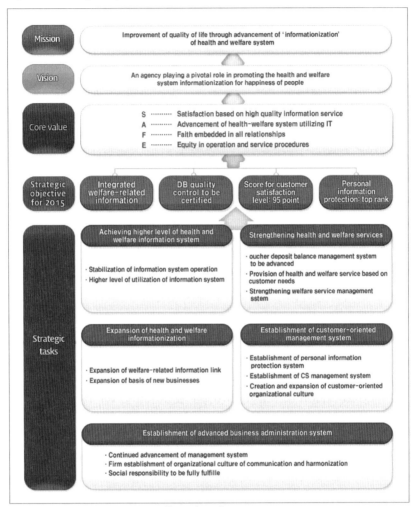

*Source: KHWIS portal site. (http://www.khiws.or.kr/eng/)

This institution basically aims to computerize social welfare administration as well as manage the welfare service voucher-related tasks, and
operating other social service administration functions in an efficient and
effective manner based on Articles 2, 6-3, and 33-7 of the Social Welfare

Services Act. KHWIS also supports the health and social welfare administration by handling the computerization of the health and medical systems based on Articles 53, 54, 56, and 57 of the Framework Act on Health and Medical Services. (KHWIS 2013, KHWIS portal site)

The mission, vision, core values, and specific strategic tasks of KHWIS as summarized in Figure 6-6. KHWIS (KHWIS homepage) have five primary tasks. The first task is to operate and manage various health and welfare information systems, including the Social Welfare Integrated Management Network (Integrated Social Welfare Management Network), the Social Welfare Facilities Information System, the Health Institutions Integrated Information System, and the Health and Welfare Portals. Secondly, KHWIS is in charge of supporting the digitization of health and welfare services as well as the digitization of the central, local, public, and private health and welfare services. KHWIS is also responsible for identifying the digital demand for the health and welfare administration as well as supporting any necessary standardization for digitization in this area.

Thirdly, KHWIS handles the integrated management of voucher-related functions for social and childcare services. This includes all the tasks involving handling voucher information and service systems for social and childcare services which are involved in paying, settling, and maintaining various vouchers. The institute also conducts research and training activities for the purpose of improving the quality of voucher programs for the social and childcare services. Fourthly, the institute analyzes and examines the various social welfare-related data that it holds, and produces related statistics which are often used to evaluate social welfare policies.

In order to effectively accomplish these tasks, the president of KHWIS initiated the organization of nine major divisions which are in charge of different areas of main operations: business planning, social services, research and development, customer support, welfare information, digitization development, welfare information, childcare services, medical and healthcare services, and information protection. The 9 divisions are supervised by the head of the Information Support Office. KHWIS has about 287 full-time employees and 220 contracted employees (KHWIS homepage).

Figure 6-7. Organizational Chart of KHWIS

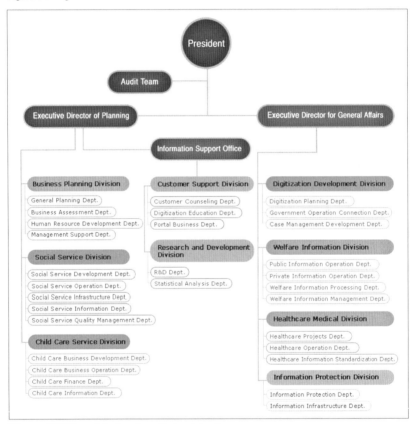

*Source: KHWIS portal site.(http://www.khwis.or.kr/eng/)

6. Major Technical Issues for the Development of SWIMN[22]

1) Integration of Databases by Resident Identification Number

One of the essential parts of integrating different databases is finding a common linking point. Fortunately, the Korean government assigned a Unique Resident Number to each individual based upon his or her birth registration. This Unique Resident Number is systematically managed by the government. This has allowed the Korean government to easily integrate different databases and different services because any piece of personal information can be identified by the Unique Identification Number; each piece of information can be merged and integrated based on the number.

2) Standardization of Income and Property

One of the core elements of SWIMN is to manage various pieces of information, such as income, property, social service, and other related information, which are used for the selection of beneficiaries and the decision of benefits paid to individuals and households. It is important to calculate standardized income based on income and property. If different service programs apply different criteria, then SWIMN cannot function. This standardization issue became an important technical problem. For this reason, SWIMN required the standardization of income and property to be integrated into different databases and different social welfare services.

....
22. This informationis taken from the White Paper on the Social Welfare Integrated Information ManagementNetwork. (MHWS. 2011)

There are five key elements to be considered for standardization. They include: 1) the number of items used for measuring income and property; 2) the operational definition of income and property; 3) the operational method for measuring income and property; 4) the assigned value for each item for income and property calculation; 5) the formula for calculating income and property for standardized income.

First of all, there was substantial variation in the number of items considered for the eligibility decisions of different social welfare programs. For example, the Basic Life Security Program considered 20 items when screening eligible beneficiaries; however, the Childcare Assistance Program and the Basic Elderly Pension Program considered 25 items and 16 items, respectively. In addition to the identification criteria for the number of items considered as income and property, a critical issue was how to estimate such income as small business earnings or daily labour wages which were not easily identified by public documents. This became an even more challenging task because different social welfare programs had different operational definitions of income and property. For example, pay for unused annual vacation is included in the Basic Elderly Pension Program and the Childcare Assistance Program as income but not in the Basic Life Security Program.

There was also inconsistency about how individual income and property are measured. For example, the Basic Elderly Pension Program calculates level of income based on data from the National Pension Service or the National Health Insurance Service if no information from the National Pension Service Basic Life Security Program is available. If the income information is not available from both agencies, then the program uses information from the National Tax Service. The Childcare Assistance Program, however, refers to data from the National Health Insurance Service and then refers to the

National Pension Service if information from the National Health Insurance Service is not available. The Basic Life Security Program did not even have any specific criteria for the calculation of income. In this case, how property was calculated for the estimation of individual income was most likely at the discretion of local government officials. SWIMN developed a method to standardize income and property for the system by reaching an agreement among agencies in charge of different social welfare programs. SWIMN also assigned basic values for different items for income calculation, but allowed different programs the flexibility to assign different weights to each item in order to reflect the unique nature of each program.

3) The Unification of Similar Document Forms

In order to make SWIMN more customer-friendly, the government simplified application forms and unified similar document forms. This allowed the applicant to apply for all the eligible programs with a minimal number of applications. Integrating 37 forms, the Korean government developed one application form (the Social Welfare Service and Pay Application Form). This single form combined the applications for more than 100 social welfare programs and with five supplementary forms (the Form for Agreement for Financial Information, the Form for Changes in Social Welfare Service and Pay, the Guaranteed Cost Payment Form, Appeal Form, and the Social Welfare Service Voucher Application Form).

7. Human Resources Development for SWIMN

Effective utilization of a system is as important as the development of the system itself. Fully utilizing the capacity of the new e-Government system is always a major objective. To maximize the utility of the new e-Government system, the government should carefully design and prepare training programs for those who are not familiar with the new system. When SWIMN was introduced, the Korean government offered training programs to different local governments. After the KHWIS took charge of the system, KHWIS provided intensive training programs. The training was offered even before the system began to operate in order to prepare local government officials to feel comfortable and ready for the new system. Between September, 2009 and December, 2009, KHWIS offered 636 training sessions and trained 24,688 government officials with a basic introduction to SWIMN and the use of its basic functions. When the system began operation in 2010, KHWIS continued to offer 774 training sessions and trained 18,006 local government officials during the first half of the year. The training sessions aimed at training people on how to use SWIMN and how to manage income and property information. Since June of 2010, KHWIS has offered 636 training sessions that have trained 24,688 local government officials. KHWIS has been committed to meeting the training needs of local government officials and has continued to offer related sessions to those who are in need. Training teams often visit local governments and offer customized training programs to those who have special training needs. For example, training teams gave additional 4-day training sessions to local government officials which were slow in managing various related information.

As the table suggests, KHWIS often offers targeted training programs when a new system is introduced. For example, KHWIS offered many programs, particularly regarding the Disability Pension Programs when the Disabilities Pension Program was officially launched in July, 2010. Most of

Table 6-4. Training Sessions in 2011

Training	Trainees	No. of Trainees	Freq.
How to use	Data management	18,006	774
New Changes	SWIMN usage	5,009	47
Additional Training Sessions	Specific functions of SWIMN	3,520	3,520
Regular Training Sessions	SWIMNusage	922	45
Regular Training Sessions	SWIMN	1,360	93
Trainings for Pension for disabilities	Pension for disabilities	963	25
Regular Training Sessions	SWIMN	325	22
Pension for disabilities	Pension for disabilities	2,875	177
Regular Training Sessions	SWIMN	1,320	49

*Source: MHWS (2011: 93-94)

the training programs offer specific content and procedural aspects which cover different stages of counsel, application, investigation, decision-making, and benefit pay, among others.

8. Lessons Moving Forward

This report gives an overall review of the emerging significance of welfare administration in the Asian-Pacific region. Though governments continue to expand their expenditures on social welfare programs, they are not quite ready for e-Government applications. E-Government is presented as a powerful solution for the improvement of efficiency, effectiveness, and transparency of social welfare administration. Based on the case study of the Korea Health and Social Welfare Information Management Network, this study offers a concise review and structural description of SWIMN.

This study also reviews the legal and institutional background of SWIMN development as well as organizational and technical issues experienced in the course of SWIMN development. This case study highlights several important lessons for those who are planning to establish a seamless and integrated social welfare information system.

- To establish a Social Welfare Integrated Management Network, unique individual identification is critical. Without a unique identification number, the integration of different databases and different social welfare services is almost impossible. To build a seamless and integrated e-Government system, the government should develop unique identification numbers and use them as a linking pin for the integration.
- A legal and institutional framework needs to be structured. The introduction of a new system requires detailed planning and needs a legal framework to support it. The legal framework needs to be carefully prepared to achieve strategic goals and strategies, including identifying participating actors, assigning decision authority and responsibility, allocating financial resources, setting timetables, etc. It is also important to establish a promotion and implementation organization which is responsible for the project. In the case of SWIMN, KHWIS was established as an organizational apparatus to establish and manage the system.
- Political leadership is imperative. The integration of different systems requires inter-agency collaboration. Inter-agency tension and conflict needs to be overcome. In the case of SWIMN, the project was identified to be a key part of the national agenda, as demonstrated by the president pledging to implement system in the presidential election. Because the SWIMN project was designated to be a priority project,

the necessary financial and political resources could be mobilized in the course of system development.

- Overcoming inter-agency conflicts is essential. Many agencies express different positions reflecting their own vested interests. SWIMN involved various agencies which held different types of public information that needed to be integrated. The role of the Prime Minister's Office in building a consensus and agreement was critical to successfully developing the system.

- Standardization is also critical in integrating different service systems. As discussed in the previous section, different social welfare programs applied different items as criteria for income and property calculation. In order to effectively operate the integrated social welfare system, standardization of income and property should be determined and implemented.

- Financial resources should be secured to implement the e-Government project. Just as with any e-Government project, it is essential to mobilize financial resources to effectively establish the planned system.

- Any e-Government project should be pursued as part of a larger e-Government vision. It should be systematically linked with other e-Government projects to maximize the potential synergistic effect.

- Human resources development is critical. Utilization of a system is more important than planning and establishment of the system. Training programs need to be prepared and structured as part of project development. Prior to operation of the system, users should have sufficient training opportunities to avoid any potential confusion or resistance to the new system.

Note: This article was funded by and reported to Korea Eximbank in 2012.

References

Baulch, B.& Weber, A. & Wood, J. (2008).*Social Protection Index for Committed Poverty Reduction:Vol. 2*, Manila: ADB.

ILO.(2010).*World Social Security Report 2010/11*. International Labour Office-Geneva.

Jung, Y.C. (2011). The Current Status and Challenge of Korea Social Welfare Informatization. *Health and Welfare Forum*, 176: 56-70.

Korea Health and Welfare Information Service (KHWIS). (2011). *Korea Health and Welfare Information Service Brochure*. Seoul. KHWIS. (www.khwis.or.kr/eng/main.do).

Ministry of Health and Welfare Service, MHWS. (2011).*WhitePaperonSocialWelfareIntegratedManagementNetwork*.Seoul: Ministry of Public Administration and Security.

Ministry of Public Administration and Security, Broadcasting and Communications Commission, Ministry of Knowledge Economy. (2012).*White Paper on National Informatization*, Seoul: Ministry of Public Administration and Security and Broadcasting and Communications Commission.

Ministry of Public Administration and Security, MOPAS. (2008).*White Paper on E-Governmnet-2003-2007*,Seoul: Ministry of Public Administration and Security.

Ministry of Public Administration and Security, MOPAS.(2011). *Digital Society Development of Korea*.Seoul: Ministry of Public Administration and Security.

Social Security Administration &International Social Security Association.(2012).*Social Security Programs throughout the World(SSA Publication N0 13-11804)*. Washington, D.C: SSA.

United Nations. (2012). *E-Government Survey 2012*.

www.khwis.or.kr/eng/main.do.

http://www.ciociso.com/news/articleView.html?idxno=9538

Chapter 7

Social Security Administration Management Information System: National Health Information System in Korea

Minah Kang (Ewha Womans University)

Social Security Administration Management Information System: National Health Information System in Korea

Minah Kang (Ewha Womans University)

1. Background

Developing a national health information system (HIS) is becoming a common tool for many countries, not only in developed countries, but in many developing countries to improve the health of the nation's citizens. HIS is concerned with improving the flow of information, through electronic means, to support the delivery of health services and the management of health systems. According to the WHO Global Observatory for e-Health, it is "the use of information and communication technologies (ICT) for health" and is concerned with improving the flow of information, through electronic means, to support the delivery of health services and the management of health systems.

We have witnessed that the ICTs provided significant benefits not only in achieving health goals, but also in demonstrating what has been attained and at what cost. The HIS is becoming acknowledged as an effective tool to achieve health system goals, such as improving the nation's health, increasing efficiency and effectiveness of health care provision administration (planning, implementation, and monitoring and evaluation) and empowering citizens (patients, tax payers, and the public) and health professionals. Patients can be empowered with health information that is of high quality, reliable, affordable, and accessible.

Central to developing the national HIS is a process of developing a master plan to build a system and infrastructure to adapt and employ the latest information communication technologies (ICT) in order to provide reliable and useful information to consumers, providers, and decision makers so that they can make the best decisions regarding purchasing and consuming health products and services, and ultimately, to improve the health of its citizens.

Adopting and utilizing advanced ICTs in health becomes more critical than ever as both rapid aging of the population as well as increasing chronic diseases are making the disease patterns more diverse and complicated. At the same time, in the mist of stringent economic challenges, there are greater demands for efficient provision of health care while meeting high expectations from citizens.

The following cases show the importance of e-health in responding to the complex needs of patients.

Mr. Kim, 61 years old, visited a local clinic because of chest pain and got an x-ray exam. His doctor recommended he visit a tertiary hospital and get a more detailed check up. A few days later, when he visited the hospital, doctors found a suspected lung cancer tumour. He had a CT scan and was advised to have surgery to remove the tumour. Next month, the day before the scheduled surgery, his doctor requested that he bring his x-ray films that were taken in the past to confirm his diagnosis. It took him a few weeks to locate the x-ray films that were taken two years before on the film, the doctor located a similar sized tumour and found that the size had not grown for two years. His doctor then reversed his decision and Mr. Kim was discharged from the hospital.[23]

Here, we see that if Mr. Kim was not able to find his old x-ray films, he might have had unnecessary surgery. If the patient's records were digitalized and saved in a safe place and delivered safely through networks, then the information could be accessed from any place and at any time when necessary. We can imagine how much benefit it would provide in an emergent situation. It would not only provide a safer and more accurate service for the patients needs, but it could save his/her life. Here is another more dramatic case example.

I had congestive heart failure, and I had just switched cardiologists. My new cardiologist provided me with new medicine without cancelling my old prescriptions. As a result, I ended up accidently overdosing on my medications, which landed me in the emergency room. The emergency room didn't have access to any of my records, so the staff didn't know that I also had diabetes. I was there for hours, and I kept getting sicker because my blood sugar was dropping, but the doctors had no way of knowing what was happening. I was in such bad shape, I couldn't communicate with them.[24]

• • • • • • • •
23. Ministry of Health andWelfare. (2007). E-health Status and Future National Plans. Presentation Slides.
24. http://www.healthit.gov/profiles/multiple-disease/multiple-chronic-conditions

Without access to his own medical records, the patient was in serious danger, very close to death.

Below is another case that shows how ICTs in health can affect the life of a patient with complicated diseases.

Managing multiple conditions: I'm not a simple patient, I know that. That's why it's so important for me to have an electronic system that helps simplify the coordination of my care. In addition to multiple chronic conditions including congestive heart failure and diabetes, I have sleep apnea, two crushed vertebrae that are pushing into my spinal cord, and neuropathy in my legs. I have a lot of doctors. There's my family physician and an endocrinologist, plus an electro-cardiologist and a regular cardiologist. And I have a defibrillator and a pacemaker – I'm practically running on batteries. So sharing my health data between so many doctors is crucial. EHRs make accessing and sharing my health information easy. That's one less thing I have to worry about. When I visit my doctors who have EHRs, it's so comforting to sit down and have the doctor immediately pull up my medical information, including current and historical data. Everything is right in front of my doctor: my past symptoms, treatments, etc. Even better, the chance of mistakes with prescriptions is minimal.[25]

According to the WHO report, each party can benefit from the HIS advancement in the following ways.

---

25. http://www.healthit.gov/profiles/multiple-disease/multiple-chronic-conditions

Table 7-1. Examples of the Benefits of HIS

Stakeholder	Impact
Citizens/ patients	Enables personalized care, throughout the health system and across the lifespan Makes health care available at home, at work or in school – not just the hospital or clinic Focuses on prevention, education and self-management Facilitates reaching out to peers for advice and support Assists mobility of citizens and their medical records Providing patient information when and where needed
Govern- ments	Delivers more reliable, responsive and timely reporting on public health; as health becomes increasingly central to economy, security, foreign affairs and international relationships. evidence-based policy decision making Creates enabling environments rather than technology limitations. Offers new roles for stakeholders, health professionals, authorities, citizens and others. Identifies disease and risk factor trends; analyses demographic, social and health data; models diseases in populations
Hospitals, academia and public health	Establishes hospitals as a virtual network of providers, connecting all levels of the system Monitors quality and safety; improves care processes and reduces the possibility of medical errors Extends collaboration and shared computing power (e.g. grid and cloud computing) Delivers services despite distance and time barriers Standardizes ordering and delivery of drugs and supplies
Professionals in research and practice	Gives access to current, specialized, accredited knowledge for clinical care, research and public health; and to research, publications and databases Enables communication between patients and providers Makes high-quality distance learning for basic and continuing professional education readily available Allows remote consultations with patients, for second opinions, and with professional Networks Opens new opportunities in basic and applied research; from health knowledge to policy and action

*Source: National eHealth Strategy Toolkit (2012). Part 1: eHealth Vision.

2. Major Programs in the Korea National HIS Master Plan

In 2005, the Korean government developed a national HIS master plan under a vision of "providing convenient and efficient health care for any person in any places through a national health information system." (Figure 7-1). The plan first and foremost pursed construction of the basic infrastructure of the HIS, such as creating laws on health information system and institutions (e.g., HIS promotion committee, Center for Interoperable EMR (electronic medical record), a Center for Public Health and Medical information, as well as a Korean Health and Wealth Information Service). At the same time, standardization of medical terms and concepts as well as promoting interoperability was another critical infrastructure upon which the HIS could perform and achieve its goals.

Figure 7-1. Korea National HIS Roadmap

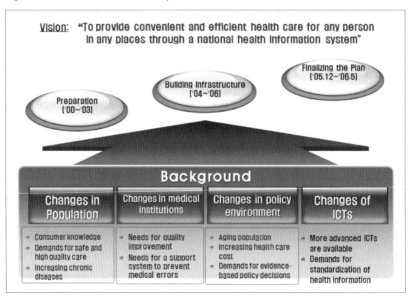

Based on these infrastructures, the Korean government launched several programs including the following three programs, namely, 1) Health Institutions Integrated Information System (HIIIS), 2) Informatization on Public Health and Medical Institutions, and 3)Integrated Disease Reporting System. Brief descriptions of the three programs follow below.

1) Health Institutions Integrated Information System (HIIIS)

The HIIIS is a program that was created to develop a standardized digital information system in around 3,500 public health centers in Korea. The system was created to support electronic administration, thus to advance technologies in place such as EMR (Electronic Medical Record) and web-based PACS (Picture Archiving Communication System), and enable electronic information exchanges by linking relevant organizations. Among the many features, the system has a function to produce health statistics automatically which will be used in health policy development. With the features, the system has contributed to increasing efficiency of hospitals and quality of health care services.

This program was created to provide various benefits to multiple parties in the society. Citizens can receive improved administrative services via the public health portal any-time and any place that they want. Health institutions can work at a higher level of productivity and achieve higher user-satisfaction through automated and continuous data collection and analysis. The government can improve policy decision making via evidence-based policy decision-making processes and implement the decisions more effectively. Finally, health systems can provide better services by cooperation and collaboration between institutions and agencies.

The program started in 2006 with a plan to informatize and link all public health centers in Korea with a web-based standardized information system and now is in the stage of stabilizing the system and providing a comprehensive and integrated public health service through the integrated health promotion management system services.

In particular, this program was created to resolve the persistent problems of the previous individual programs, such as inefficiencies and low consumer satisfaction from duplication in the working process, manual handling of customer applications, and the lack of linkage betwen institutions. Therefore, this new program was expected to provide better, safer, and more convenient services to patients, to lower the operation cost of public health centers, to increase convenience through electronic public health services, to simplify the working process for public managers, and to

Figure 7-2. Public Health Portal

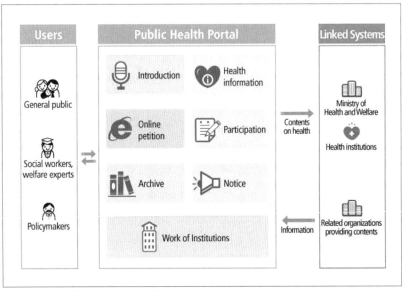

*Source: KHWIS. Korean Health and Welfare Information Service Brochure.
http://www.khwis.or.kr/eng/pageFwr.do?sd=PS&ms=21020000.

reduce the inequalities between individual health centers. Furthermore, the government can achieve a policy making a process more effectively through feedback from automated data collection and analysis.

Among the various features of the HIIIS, the public health portal(http:// phi.mw.go.kr) deserves a special note (Figure 7-2). The portal system was created in 2007 to provide an on-line public health services to the public. The system provides various types of easy-to-understand health information to the public using video clips and animation. It offers information on health issues and self-diagnosis tips for multiple diseases, as well as allowing the citizens to search for public health centers that are near to their home. Citizens can make an appointment with a doctor, retrieve their medical history, and request to issue their own medical records on-line such as immunization certificates. Figure 7-2 shows the major functions of the public health portal as well as how the system interacts with users and links to other health systems.

2) Informatization on Public Health and Medical Institutions

The Public health institution informatization Project is a project that aims to improve the performance of public health institutions and hospitals and their medical services by advancing the hospital information system and electronically linking public hospitals with each other. It is intended to be a pilot project in the public sector which can be extended to an integrated hospital information system in Korea including those in the private sector. This project starts with establishing and adopting advanced ICTs in various public health service areas. Establishing the EMR system is a key program which would allow patients to access their medical records easily and conveniently at any place and any time when they need it. The project is expected to improve the services of public hospitals in Korea, to improve their levels of efficiency and performance. At the same time, it is expected to provide more services to people and places that were marginalized because of geographic or socio-economic reasons.

3) Integrated Disease Reporting System

The Korean Center of Diseases Control and Prevention has launched the integrated disease reporting system, which is a timely response to the rising public health problems and hazards because of rapid changes in citizens' life styles, increasing mobilization of population, and the aging population. New infectious diseases and prevalent chronic diseases are becoming serious public health concerns. This project is expected to perform a rigorous surveillance of these new risks and hazards and to provide effective responses to those risks by collecting and analysing data, and providing information to the public so that the citizens can prevent and respond to the risks in an effective and timely manner.

More specifically, the major goals of the project are 1) to quickly respond to occurrence of infectious diseases, 2) to support preventive research and programs, 3) to maximize productivity of public health interventions and disease information utilization, and 4) support consumer oriented life-course health management.

3. Legal and Institutional Backgrounds for Introduction of Informatization on Health and Medical Services

1) Legal Bases for Health Institutions Integrated Information System (HIIIS)

Legal bases to support projects for informatization on health and medical institutions can be mainly found in the following three laws: (1) The Framework Act on Health and Medical Services, (2) The Regional Public Health Act, and (3) The Health and Medical Service Technology Promotion Act. Details of relevant provisions under these laws are as set forth below.

(1) The Framework Act on Health and Medical Services <Act No. 10131 Mar. 17, 2010>

- Major Provisions
    - Article 54 (Facilitation of Informatization on Health and Medical Services). The State and local governments shall formulate necessary policies to facilitate the informatization of health and medical services.
    - Article 56 (Dissemination and Expansion of Information on Health and Medical Services). The Minister for Health and Welfare Affairs shall formulate necessary polices to disseminate and expand information on health and medical services held by health and medical institutions and the relevant institutions or organizations, etc.
    - Article 57 (Facilitation of Standardization of Information on Health and Medical Services). The Minister for Health and Welfare Affairs shall formulate policies to standardize the information on health and medical services, in order to efficiently operate information on

health and medical services and secure compatibility, etc.

- Legislation History, Purpose and Summary

The Framework Act on Health and Medical Services (the "Act"), which is one of the major legal bases for informatization on health and medical institutions, was enacted in Jan. 12, 2000 and has been enforced since July 13, 2000 with several amendments.

Pursuant to Article 1 of the Act, the purpose of the Act is "to prescribe the rights and duties of nationals and the obligations of the State and local governments, with regard to health and medical services, and provide for basic matters on the supply of and demand for health and medical services, thereby contributing to the development of health and medical services and the improvement of national health and welfare."

Composed of a total of fifty seven articles, the Act stipulates obligations of the State and local governments as well as health and medical personnel, and duties and rights of patients. For instance, Chapter II (Rights and Duties of Nationals Concerning Health and Medical Services) of the Act, which consists of articles from Article 10 to Article 14, specifies people's rights to health, rights to know about health and medical services that they receive, patient's rights for guarantee of their confidentiality, and people's duties not to harm the health of others and to cooperate with health and medical services personnel when required. In addition, Chapter III (Formulation and Implementation of Plans on Development of Health and Medical Services) of the Act, which consists of articles from Article 15 to Article 23, emphasizes the obligations of the State and local governments to formulate and implement plans every five years for the purpose of contribution to the development of health and medical services, and to cooperate with one another and also with the relevant administrative agencies as well as public and private health and medical institutions. Furthermore, Section 3 (System of Managing Major Diseases) of Chapter V (Provision and Use of Health and Medical Services) of the Act constitutes provisions to support establishment of systems to manage major diseases, and Chapter VII (Management of Statistics and Information on Health and Medical Services) of the Act constitutes provisions for proper management of statistics and information on the relevant health and medical services.

(2) Regional Public Health Act <Act No. 9847 Dec. 29, 2009>

- Major Provision
  - Article 2 (Responsibilities of State and Local Governments). (1) The State shall strive to survey and research regional health and medical care, to collect, arrange, and apply information, to train and improve the quality of human resources; and shall devise policies of extending technical and financial support necessary for the establishment and enforcement of health policies of the Seoul Special Metropolitan City, Metropolitan Cities and Dos (hereinafter referred to as the "City/ Do" and Si/Gun/Gu (hereinafter limited to an autonomous Gu). (2)(3) [intentionally omitted]

- Legislation History, Purpose and Summary

Regional Public Health Act (the "Act"), the formerly Public Health Clinics Act enacted and enforced in 1956, was wholly amended on Dec. 29, 1995 and has been enforced since July 1, 1996 with several amendments.

Pursuant to Article 1 of the Act, the Act aims "to contribute to the improvement of national health through reasonable organization and operation of the health administration and through effective execution of health policies, providing matters necessary for the establishment and operation of regional health and medical institutions such as public health clinics, and for the purpose of securing a co-relationship of regional health and medical services."

The Act articulates responsibilities of the State and local governments, establishment of medical care plans for regional public health, enforcement and evaluation of the plans and additional provisions on public health clinics.

(3) Health and Medical Service Technology Promotion Act <Act No. 10996, Aug. 4, 2011>

- Major Provisions
  - Article 3 (Protection and Fosterage of Technology Development). The government shall establish and execute the policy for encouragement, protection and fostering of the research and development activities for promotion of health and medical service technology and the new technology in health service, and may support the necessary expenses.
  - Article 10 (Promotion of Health and Medical Service Information). The Minister of Health and Welfare shall promote the Projects under the following subparagraphs for the production, circulation, and utilization of health and medical service information: 1. Fosterage of specialized research institutions for the management of health and medical service information; 2. Research, development and management concerning the standards of affairs for the promotion of computerization in the field of health and medical service and welfare; 3. Activation of joint utilization of health and medical service information; and 4. Other important activities for the promotion of health and medical service information as prescribed by Ordinance of the Ministry of Health and Welfare.

• Legislation History, Purpose and Summary

The Health and Medical Service Technology Promotion Act (the "Act") was enacted on Dec. 6, 1995 and has been enforced since March 7, 1996 with several amendments.

Pursuant to Article 1 of the Act, the Act aims "to contribute to the sound development of the health and medical services industry and the promotion of the national health by establishing the basic plan for promotion of health and medical services technology, performing the research and development activities for health and medical service technology, prescribing the matters concerning certification of new technology in health service and health and medical service information, etc. and establishing the Korean Health and Medical Service Research Institute performing the analysis on health and medical service technology, etc."

2) Legal Bases for Informatization on Public Health and Medical Institutions

Projects to support informatization on public health and medical institutions are mainly based on the following laws and relevant policies as set forth below.

(1) Framework Act on Health and Medical Services <Act No. 10131 Mar. 17, 2010>

- Article 54 (Facilitation of Informatization on Health and Medical Services). The State and local governments shall formulate necessary policies to facilitate the informatization of health and medical services.

(2) Public Health and Medical Services Act <Act. 11247 Feb. 1, 2012>

- Major Provision
  - Article 6 (Establishment of Operation of Public Health and Medical Institutions). (1)The State and local governments shall endeavor to meet the national basic demand for public health and medical services in an equitable manner by establishing and operating public health and medical institutions. (2) The State and local governments may subsidize expenses incurred in establishing and operating public health and medical institutions.

- Legislation History, Purpose and Summary

The Public Health and Medical Services Act (the "Act") was enacted on Jan. 12, 2000 and has been enforced since July 13, 2000 with several amendments, including the most recent one in Feb. 1, 2012 that will enter into force as of Feb. 2, 2013.

Pursuant to Article 1 of the Act, the Act aims "to efficiently provide high quality public health and medical services to nationals and ultimately contribute to the improvement of national health by providing for basic matters on public health and medical services."

The Act reflects the concept of equity in provision of public health and medical services. For instance, Article 7 of the Act is a preferential provision to give priority to particularly vulnerable populations for provision of medical services. The Act mainly covers various matters on evaluation of public health and medical institutions and training of employees of the relevant institutions.

3) Legal Bases for Establishment of Integrated Disease Reporting System for Korean Centers for Diseases Control and Prevention

Projects to establish an integrated intelligence system for the Korean Centers for Disease Control and Prevention are mainly based on the following laws, guidelines and instructions as set forth below.

(1) Framework Act on National Informatization <Act No. 10629 May 19, 2011>

- Major Provision
  - Article 15 (Promotion of Public Informatization). (1) National agencies, etc. shall promote the informatization of the affairs under their competence, such as administration, health, social welfare, education, culture, environment, science, technology, etc. for purposes of raising the efficiency of administrative affairs and furthering the benefit of the nation. (2) National agencies, etc. shall prepare necessary measures, such as the introduction and use of information technology architecture, and other measures for the purpose of efficiently promoting informatization under paragraph (1) (hereinafter referred as "public informatization").

- Legislation History, Purpose and Summary

Framework Act on National Informatization (the "Act"), formerly the Framework Act on Informatization Promotion enacted in 1995 and enforced in 1996, was wholly amended on May 22, 2009 and has been enforced since Aug. 23, 2009 with several amendments.

Pursuant to Article 1 of the Act, the Act aims "to contribute to the realization of a sustainable knowledge and information based society, and to improve the quality of life for the nation by prescribing matters necessary for the establishment and promotion of the basic direction of national informatization and policies relevant thereto."

The Act has significant implications on health and medical services informatization. Section 1 (Promotion of Informatization by Sector) of Chapter III (Promotion of National Informatization), which consists of articles from Article 15 to Article 24, emphasizes the importance of promoting public and community informatization, sharing and distribution of knowledge and information, cooperating with private sectors and international societies, and promoting standardization. In addition, Section 1 (Guaranteeing Soundness and Universality in the Use of Information) of Chapter IV (Prevention of Adverse Effects of National Informatization) includes provisions to reduce negative effects due to informatization: for instance, narrowing the digital divide and increasing access to information particularly for people with disabilities, aged persons, etc. The Act also spares some parts to ensure the guarantee of safety and reliability in the use of information.

(2) Infectious Disease Control and Prevention Act <Act No. 11439, May 23, 2012>

- Major Provisions
  - Article 4 (Duties of State and Local Government). (1) The State and local government shall respect the dignity and values of patients, etc. infected by infectious diseases as human beings, protect their fundamental rights, and shall not accord them any unfavorable treatment, such as restrictions on their employment, unless otherwise provided

for in Acts. (2) [intentionally omitted]

- Article 6 (Duties and Rights of Citizens). (1) [Intentionally omitted] (2) All citizens are entitled to know information on the occurrence status of infectious disease, on the prevention, control, etc. thereof, and methods of responding thereto.

- Article 15 (Detection and Control of Patients, etc. Infected by Infectious Diseases). Where the head of a public health clinic receives a notification under Articles 11 and 12 on any patient, etc. infected by an infectious disease who lives in his/her jurisdiction, he/she shall record him/her in a register and manage the register (including using electronic documents), as prescribed by Ordinance of the Ministry of Health and Welfare.

- Article 16 (Sentinel Surveillance, etc. of Infectious Diseases). (1) (2) [intentionally omitted] (3) The Minister of Health and Welfare, a Mayor/ Do Governor or the head of a Si/Gun/Gu shall provide relevant institutions, organizations, establishments or citizens with important information on national health collected under paragraph (2). (4) [Intentionally omitted] (5) Matters necessary for the designation, etc. of infectious diseases subject to sample surveillance under paragraph (1) and of sample surveillance institutions shall be determined by Ordinance of the Ministry of Health and Welfare. (6) (7) [intentionally omitted]

- Article 18 (Epidemiological Investigation). (1) Where the Director of the Korea Centers for Disease Control and Prevention, a Mayor/ Do Governor or the head of a Si/Gun/Gu deems that an infectious disease breaks out and is likely to prevail subsequently, he/she shall immediately conduct an epidemiological investigation. (2) (3) (4) [intentionally omitted]

• Legislation History, Purpose and Summary

Infectious Disease Control and Prevention Act (the "Act"), formerly the Prevention of Contagious Diseases Act enacted in 1954 and enforced in 1957, was wholly amended on Dec. 29, 2009 and has been enforced since Dec. 30, 2010 with several amendments.

Pursuant to Article 1 of the Act, the Act aims "to contribute to the improvement and maintenance of citizens' health by preventing the occurrence and prevalence of infectious diseases hazardous to citizens' health, and prescribing necessary matters for the prevention and control thereof."

In order to prevent the prevalence of infectious diseases hazardous to citizens' health, Article 9 of the Act prescribes that an Infectious Disease Control Committee should investigate and carry out research on infectious diseases and dissemination of knowledge concerning the prevention, control, etc. of infectious diseases. Detection of patients infected by infectious diseases through epidemiological investigation as well as management of the information after examinations is also stated in the Act.

(3) **Act on the Protection of Personal Information Maintained by Public Institutions <Act No. 10142 Mar. 22, 2010>**

(4) **Others**

• Guidelines for the National Intelligence and Security (National Intelligence Service)
• Minister Instructions: enhancement of personal information security, establishment of security systems, Increase of penalties against inside leaks, etc. (July, Aug. and Nov. 2008)

4. Organizational and technical components of the e-health system in Korea

1) Health Institutions Integrated Information System (HIIIS)

The HIIIS is a program to standardize a digital information system installed in around 3,500 public health institutions including public health centers. Figure 7-3. shows how the system is structured as well as how it interacts with the public and other relevant organizations.

The intended goals of the HISS are the followings:

Figure 7-3. The Health Institutions Integrated Information System

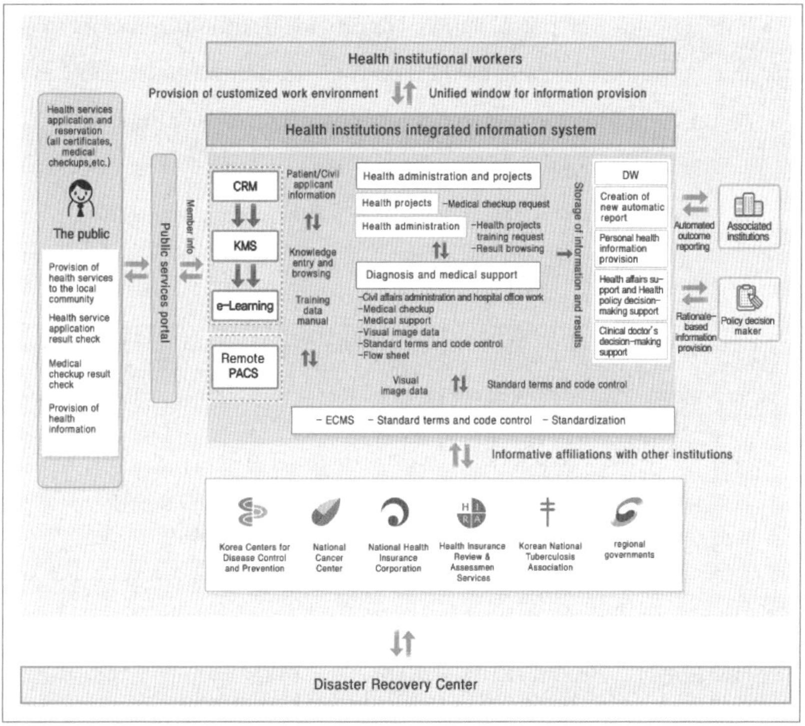

*Source: http://www.khwis.or.kr/eng/pageFwr.do?sd=PS&ms=21010400

- Support clinical services: to achieve higher efficiencies in health service provisions and supporting services by promoting EMR application, informatization of clinical and financial activities, and exchange of clinical data between health institutions.
- Informatization of public health programs and management: To promote efficiencies in public health programs by customizing the reach-out services and public health management program and projects, such as chronic disease management, infectious disease management, and health screening, etc.
- Automatization of data collection: To build the Data Warehouse (DW) and knowledge based repository (KBR), and to build a data collecting system to collect data automatically, continuously, and regularly
- Public health web portal service: To provide health information, to enable consumers to issue medical certificates, search clinics and health centers, and access to test results and clinical records on-line.

The HIIIS project was developed in the following stages (Table 7-2).

Table 7-2. HIIIS Development Stages

Stage	Development	Time Period
Preparation	Development of the Regional Public Health ISP	'04. 12 ~ '05. 10
1st Stage	Development of HIIIS S/W Conducted surveys of patients and potential users Implemented pilot programs Developed the application programs for the public health management programs, clinical EMR/clinical support system, public health portal, and the KBR	'06. 09 ~ '07. 08
2nd stage	Implemented the full scale HIIIS Refinement of the system and development of new features Build the KMS (Knowledge Management System) and the CRM(customer relationship management). Refinement of the operational environment such as IT infrastructures	'07. 09 ~ '08. 12

3rd stage	Construction of DRS (disaster recovery system) and Data Mining bases	'08. 11 ~ '09. 05
4th stage	Stabilized operation Strengthened security of the system	'09.06 ~ present

*Source: Young-Mi Chang, et al. (2011).

2) Informatization of public health institutions

The goal of this project is to develop and expand the 'next generation' hospital information system, such as the OCS (Order Communication System) and EMR (electronic medical record) in the public health institutions in Korea. Currently, this project is expanded to several public hospitals in various local areas including Seoul Public Hospital, Choonchun Public Hospital, Najoo Public Hospital, and Kongjoo Public Hospital, after a series of feasibility and validity tests as well as the two pilot programs.

Table 7-3. Stages of Informatization of Public Health Institutions

'07.09	Developed a national Public Health ISP
'07.09~'08.10	2007' public health programs health information integration system development public hospital business process re-engineering (BPR)
'08.12	feasibility and validity test about public health informatization project
'09.02~'10.10	Expand the project based on the validity and feasibility test results Implemented the 1st pilot program for the hospital information system at the Incheon Public Hospital
'10.12~	Implementing the 2nd pilot program for the hospital information system at the Pusan Public Hospital

*Source: National Information Agency (2009). https://www.nia.or.kr/files/ko/nia2009/download/ whitepaper/2009/04_01_02_03.pdf

3) Integrated Disease Reporting System for Korea Centers for Diseases Control and Prevention

The main goal of the integrated disease reporting system at the Korea CDC is to build an effective prevention and public health management system that can respond to unexpected public health emergency situations quickly and in a timely matter. The system is an integrated intelligence system where 94 internal processing programs were combined in 2007. The system also aims to improve the public's access to the system by redesigning their webpage. The system provides information on infectious diseases through their website. The system was developed through the following stages.

Table 7-4. Stages of the disease reporting system development

2007-2008.2	created a consumer oriented portal site to provide information on diseases standardization of internal operational process
2008.6-2009.4	consolidation of operational systems, connection with outside agencies and between health centers, Removal of duplicated processes Separation of intranet from external networks for security
2009.5.-2010	consolidation of specialized operations such as quarantine information systems, chronic disease surveillance systems, etc.
2010:	Itracking system for new infectious diseases Surveillance information system GIS-based disease surveillance and prevention system

*Source: Korea Centers for Diseases Control and Prevention.

Figure 7-4. Disease Reporting System of Korea CDC

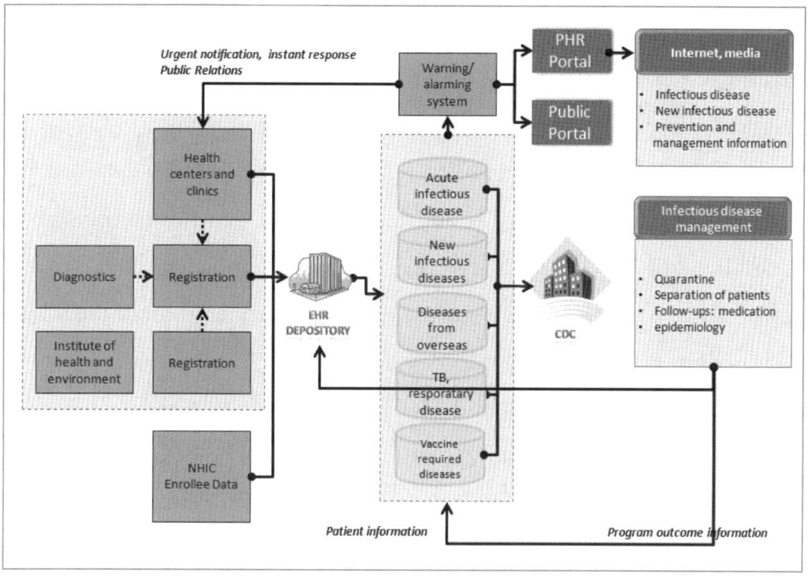

*Source: Korea Centers for Diseases Control and Prevention.

5. Human Capital Strengthening for the Korean HIS

In the final report for the 'Health Information System Development Plan in Local Areas', the Korean Ministry of Health and Welfare reports the strengths and weaknesses in the current workforce in the area of health information systems in Korea. According to them, the main strength of human capital in the public health sector in Korea is a strong willingness of the health center directors to informationize their systems. However, the report pointed out that a heavy work load and frequent transitions between jobs are causing discontinuity in workflows. Moreover, lack of relevant knowledge and maintenance problems were frequently located.

In response, the following were suggested: 1) Encouragement of active participation of the staff and workforce in informatization planning, 2) strengthening education programs of public health staff on health information systems, and 3) hiring 67 additional ICT professionals whose sole responsibility is ICT system management and development.

At the system level, the HWIS (Korea Health and Welfare Information Services) was created in 2009 to establish and operate an information system for digitalizing public health and welfare services and management systems efficiently by operating businesses to facilitate the digitization of the health and medical system in accordance with Articles 53~54 and 56~57 of the 'Framework Act on Health and Medical Services'. The HWIS has been operating the new user-friendly health service system based on digitization; such as the Health Institutions Integrated Information System.

While the HWIS performs various functions including operation and management of all health and welfare information systems, support of the digitization of health and welfare services, integrated management of voucher business for social and nurturing service, support for policy development, user service and quality management, the HWIS also manages call centers and education projects to support local civil servants in the social welfare & health department and social welfare institutions' employees who use the information system.

In particular, the Information Support Office has a Digitization Education Department within the Customer Support Division which operates a Help Center for ICT operators and education programs. Currently, the Digitization Education Department has 16 staff and performs the following tasks: 1) developing a yearly and long-term plan for education programs, 2) planning and management of education programs for system users, 3) development of curriculum and teaching materials, 4) satisfaction surveys, and 5) statistics and data collection.

In terms of program content, in the beginning, the major content of the education was to raise the level of utilization of ICTs in the area of health area. Recently, protecting privacy and security has been the major focus of the education. The Korean Human Resource Development Institute for Health and Welfare (KOHI) is providing an on-line education course on privacy protection. Also, in an effort to promote knowledge accumulation and learning on ICTs, various events and competition such as the ICT capacity competition were held. Also, there were numerous workshops and seminar programs for ICT training of public health experts and medical providers.

6. Remaining issues and future tasks for the Korea national HIS

1) Lack of a robust conceptual framework for HIS

While having already achieved several important milestones in the HIS roadmap, Korea has a number of important remaining tasks. Foremost, there is an urgent need to establish a more systematic and long-term master plan to strengthen its national HIS. Since its first initiation in 1999, the Korean government has made intensive efforts to build a nation health information system.

Nevertheless, the HIS in Korea is not yet constructed on a coherent conceptual framework that is built upon a theoretical base and reflects the core values of the society. The successful application of the ICTs does require not only sufficient knowledge and expertise in ICTs but also understanding of the values, priorities, and visions of the nation. Without such a long term road-map and framework, decision makers, providers and consumers will not be able to tailor the HIS to the country's own national values, resources, and requirements. The Conceptual framework for the HIS can serve as an umbrella for planning and coordinating different national HIS efforts while considering fundamental elements in terms of regulatory, governance, standards, human capacity, financing and policy contexts. Without a robust conceptual framework, HIS loses synergy with the healthcare system and eventually fails to achieve progress toward health system goals. Also, problems in standardization and interoperability will not receive sufficient attention. Similarly, comprehensive and coherent budget planning and allocation cannot be made without such a roadmap. Also, a governance structure and roles cannot be set up.

2) Working with stakeholders

In order to build an effective HIS that is well researched and widely sup-

Figure 7-5. Four Common Stakeholder roles in the development of a national HIS vision

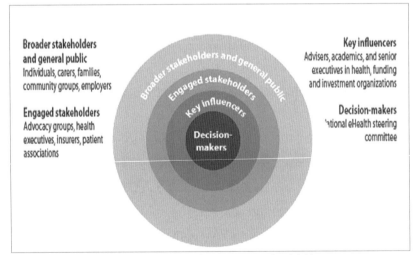

*Source: National eHealth Strategy Toolkit (2012).Chapter 5. Engage with stakeholders.

ported requires working with a range of multi-sectorial stakeholders. Those stakeholders have their own interests regarding delivery and utilization of the ICTS and health products and services. An inclusive approach that tries to work with stakeholders on a wide spectrum will build a cooperative relationship and create a common understanding on the values and priorities of the nation's health system. This engagement can be achieved with constant efforts to ensure that stakeholders' interests are understood and that they remain informed on progress. More specifically, to involve stakeholders, clarifying the goals of the national health system and HIS, identifying and understanding the stakeholder groups, developing a pragmatic approach to communicate and collaborate with these groups, and defining the points at which consultation and cooperation will occur. A PPP (Public and Private Partnership) is another form of stakeholder involvement where the public and private sectors work together in the processes of designing, planning, constructing and operating ICT projects. Examples of PPP arrangement are becoming more and more diverse.

Table 7-5. Examples of PPP arrangements

▶Operation and maintenance contract (O and M).

These projects involve the private sector operating a publicly-owned facility under contract with the government.

▶Lease, develop and operate (LDO).

This type of project involves a private developer being given a long-term lease to operate and expand existing infrastructure. The private developer agrees to invest in infrastructure improvements and can recover the investment plus a reasonable return over the term of the lease.

▶Build, operate and maintain (BOM).

This arrangement involves the private-sector developer building, owning and maintaining infrastructure. The government leases the infrastructure and operates it using public sector staff.

▶Build, own, operate and transfer (BOOT).

These projects involve a private developer financing, building, owning and operating infrastructure for a specified period. At the expiration of the specified period, the infrastructure is returned to the government.

▶Build, own and operate (BOO).

These projects operate similarly to a BOOT project, except that the private sector owns the infrastructure in perpetuity. The developer may be subject to regulatory constraints on operations and, in some cases, pricing. The long-term right to operate the infrastructure provides the developer with significant financial incentive for the capital investment in the facility.

▶Build, lease and transfer (BLT).

An arrangement whereby a concessionaire is authorized to finance and construct infrastructure, and upon its completion turn it over to the government agency or local government unit concerned on a lease arrangement for a fixed period. After this, ownership of the infrastructure is automatically transferred to the government agency or local government unit concerned.

▶Build-operate-share-transfer (BOST)

An arrangement whereby a concessionaire is authorized to finance, construct, operate and maintain, share a part of the revenue and transfer the infrastructure at the end of the period. The proponent is allowed to recover its total investment, operating and maintenance costs plus a reasonable return thereon by collecting tolls, fees, rentals or other charges from infrastructure users.

*Source: National eHealth Strategy Toolkit (2012). Annex F. Public Private Partnerships (PPPs).

3) Standardization and interoperability of health information

In order to achieve the goal of HIS, which is to provide the right health information "to the right person at the right place and time in a secure, electronic form to optimize the quality and efficiency of health care delivery, research, education and knowledge", the health information should be able to transfer between institutions and across geographical boundaries. For such information exchange, developing a system of electronic health records, patient registries and shared knowledge resources is critical. The advent of digital information and communication technologies (ICTs) did not automatically solve these problems of physical, economic, and knowledge barriers to receive optimal healthcare services. Patients living in remote areas still lacked direct access to medical professionals, and medical devices could not be electronically connected from remote locations to advanced medical facilities.

These barriers can only be overcome with e-health standards, the specifications that enable interoperability among healthcare-related information and communication technologies and systems made by different providers. Standards represent "information in common formats, encrypt or compress information, perform functions like error detection and correction, or provide common addressing or security structures."

Lack of interoperability is noted as one of the greatest threats to achieving the improvements to healthcare and cost efficiency promised by emerging e-health systems. The problem does not occur only by technical barriers but frequently a market-driven barrier arising from the economic competition, as well as the lack of incentives among healthcare delivery systems to adopt standards. Only with a critical mass of health care providers who adhere to the same standards, the reliable and interoperable sharing of information over communication networks and between devices is possible.

Table 7-6. illustrates common standards and interoperability components. Without these components, health information cannot be collected consistently, will be open to misinterpretation, and will be difficult or impossible to share due to incompatibilities in data structures and terminologies.

Table 7-6. Common Standards and Interoperability components

Component	Description	Examples
Data Structure Standards	These standards govern the way health datasets are stored using consistent data structure and can be presented with consistency in software applications, to ensure information is neither misinterpreted nor overlook.	Referrals and specialist letters Health event summaries Prescriptions, test orders and results Care plans Real-time clinical data Appointments Electronic health records
Common terminologies	These enable information communicated electronically to make use of a common language for describing symptoms, diagnoses and treatments.	Clinical coding standards Medical terminology standards Medicines terminology standards
Messaging standards	These define message structure to allow data to be transmitted and received through the secure messaging infrastructure from one care provider to another. They also define the acknowledgements that should be provided when a message is delivered or opened and the warnings to be generated if the message is not delivered, or is declined.	Message structures Message transmission protocols Message acknowledgement protocols
Secure messaging standards	These are for the secure transmission and delivery of messages and the appropriate authentication of the message receiver, to ensure that information is securely transmitted and delivered to the correct recipient.	Privacy andconfidentiality Authentication Non-repudiation
Software accreditation standards	These define the criteria with which eHealth software products and services must comply in order to be certified as able to exchange health information with the national eHealth environment.	Quality Security Interoperability

*Source: National eHealth Strategy Toolkit (2012). Chapter 9. Identify the required eHealth components.

4) Protection of individual privacy and promote security of personal information

Perhaps, the two most critical components of medical information exchange are "protecting security" and "standardization of information."

With development and accumulation of health information, protecting privacy and securely saving the information becomes a critical issue. Due to the inherently sensitive nature of the patient information, requiring a high degree of privacy protections, quality assurance, and security is one of the most keen HIS policy issues. Building the highest levels of security for data integrity, access controls, and authentication of users is demanded. However, protecting privacy and security can conflict with needs for standards and interoperability in health ICTs policy decisions. Efforts have to weigh the requirements (legal and social) for protecting the individual privacy of patients and patient data as well as promoting standards and interoperability possibility.

The 2003 legislation in Japan specifies that for transfer of patients' medical records, even among clinical providers for the purpose of diagnoses and treatment, it is necessary to obtain patients' consent before the transfer. Protection of patients' records are not only important to protect patients' privacy, but can be used as important evidence for medical error litigations, so safely and securely saving it, protecting it, and transferring patient information is a critical matter.

5) Monitoring and evaluation of HIS development and implementation

Monitoring and evaluation of HIS activities and outcomes becomes a critical component of successful development and implementation of HIS. It involves tracking and assessing the validity and appropriateness of the HIS plans and the results of implementing the HIS action plans. In order to monitor and evaluate the progress and identify inhibiting barriers to successful implementation of HIS, performances and processes should be defined with measurable indicators, baselines, and targets. Table 7-7. presents criteria for selecting M&E indicators.

Table 7-7. Suggested Criteria for selection M&E indicators

Criteria	Meaning
Linked to objectives	Indicators should provide information that can be linked to and support the monitoring and evaluation of eHealth outcomes and outputs
Quantifiable	Indicators should be concrete, as opposed to conceptual, and should be measurable and easily expressed in relevant units of measurement
Observable	Measurement data exists (or will exist) that will allow an indicator to be derived
Reliable	The data used for the indicators should not be arbitrarily derived and should reflect accurate, verifiable information as much as is possible
Controllable	Indicators should measure the results of delivering the eHealth action plan, and should be selected to control the potential impact of activities that fall outside the scope of the plan
Ongoing and comparable	Indicators should provide information that is comparable and relevant across periods, rather than being 'one time' indicators of progress

*Source: National eHealth Strategy Toolkit (2012). Part 3: Monitoring and Evaluation.

7. Conclusion: Recommendation and Implication

HIS is a means to ensure that "the right health information is provided to the right person at the right place and time in a secure, electronic form to optimize the quality and efficiency of health care delivery, research, education and knowledge." Building a national HIS becomes more critical than ever, with increasing pressure from ageing population and the advent of new and prevalent infectious and chronic diseases. Without an effective HIS, a nation's health care system cannot scale up to support a larger patient and care provider base. While HIS is a priority for health system development, it should be incorporated as a strategic and integrated action at the national level. Otherwise, duplication of efforts will lead to inefficient allocation of resources and inhibit implementation of integrating solutions. With small scale applications, it would be impossible to achieve a goal of effectively communicating and sharing information with other health systems or across geographies, technologies or programs. Only by incorporating the HIS at the national level, collaboration between the health and ICT sectors, and both public and private can be achieved.

HIS at the national level should aim to achieve the following objectives. Most basically, the HIS should allow the shift from paper-based to computer-based processing and storage, as well as the increase of data in health care settings. At the same time, it will bring the shift from institution-centered departmental and, later, hospital information systems towards regional and global HIS. The system can promote the inclusion of patients and health consumers as HIS users, besides health care professionals and administrators. The HIS data can be used not only for patient care and administrative purposes, but also for health care planning as well as clinical and epidemiological research. The HIS aims to achieve the shift from focusing mainly on technical HIS problems to those of change management as well as of strategic information management, as well as the shift from mainly alphanumeric data in HIS to images and now also to data on the molecular level. Finally, the steady increase of new technologies is now starting to include ubiquitous computing environments and sensor-based technologies for health monitoring.

By all means, a successful HIS should enhance the level of health and welfare of the citizens by standardizing work related to health, with one-stop digitized systems that are convenient and accessible to users, and ensuring people's opportunities to benefit from health services regardless of their socioeconomic status and geographical locations. By applying digital technologies to health and welfare systems, HIS should aim to make the delivery of the essential health services more efficient.While the HIS of a nation cannot solve all the problems and issues of a health system, it has a great potential to assist the system to run more equally, effectively and efficiently.

Note: This article was funded by and reported to Korea Eximbank in 2012.

References

Chang, Young-Mi. et al. (2011). A study on Implementing Local Specialized Public Health Service to Public Health Information System. KHWIS.

Choi, Jeong-A& Kim, Yeonhee. (2011). Success Factors for an Integrated Information Systemfor Health Centers. *Journal of Korean Association for Regional Information Society,*14(1):73-92.

Hillestad, R., Bigelow, J., Bower, A., Girosi, F., Meili, R., Scoville, R., & Taylor, R. (2005). Can electronic medical record systems transform health care? Potential health benefits, savings, and costs. *Health Affairs,* 24(5), 1103-1117.

Hwang, J. Ryu, S. &Jeong, B. (2006) *A Study on the Stages Diagnosis of It Health Care.*National Information Society Agency.

Healy, J. C. (2008). Implementing e-health in developing countries: Guidance and principles. *ICT Applications and Cybersecurity Division CYB, White Paper, September.*

Jeun, Young-ju. (2007). A Study on Revising the Medical Law for Medical Record InformationManagement. *Law-studies,*28: 465-483.

Kim, Y., Bae, J., Kwak, M.&Joo, Y. (2007). *Development Plan for National HealthInformation System in Korea.* Center for Interoperable EHR.

Kim, Yeo-Ra. (2010). Exploring the Social and Legal Issues of Internet Medical Information: Focusing on the Credibility of Internet Medical Information Use and Invasion of Cyber-Privacy. *Communication Science Research,*10(2): 179-220.

Lee, Sang-Myeong. (2008). The Medical Treatment Informatization and Medical TreatmentInformation Protection.*Law Review,* 25(1): 39-56.

Ministry of Health and Welfare. (2010-2012). *Ministry of Health and Welfare White Paper.*

Ministry of Health Welfare and Family Affairs. (2010-2012).*Promotion Plan for E-Health.*

Murray, E., May, C., &Mair, F. (2010). Development and formative evaluation of the e-Health Implementation Toolkit (e-HIT). *BMC medical informatics and decision making, 10*(1), 61.

World Health Organization. (2006). Building foundations for ehealth. *Progress of Member States, Report of the WHO Global Observatory for ehealth.*

Park, Joohi. (2010). *Investigative Analysis on the Promotion and Development Direction of Information in Healthcare.* Samyook University.

Payne, T. H., Bates, D. W., Berner, E. S., Bernstam, E. V., Covvey, H. D., Frisse, M. E., ... &Ozbolt, J. (2012). Healthcare information technology and economics. *Journal of the American Medical Informatics Association*, amiajnl-2012.

Policy & Technology Watch Division. (2012). *E-Health Standards and Interoperability Itu-Technology Watch Report. In ITU-T Technology Watch.* Geneva: ITU Telecommunica-tionStandardization Bureau.

World Health Organization. (2012). *National eHealth strategy toolkit.* International Tele-communication Union.

Chapter 8

Information Villages in Korea

Moon-Gi Jeong (Sungkyunkwan University)

Information Villages in Korea

Moon-Gi Jeong (Sungkyunkwan University)

1. Introduction

The development of Information and Communication Technology (ICT) has made knowledge and information one of the significant assets for the national and local development as well as the increase of living standards (Drucker, 1999). This change in ICT increased the digital divide among the urban and rural regions. As the digital divide exacerbated depending on regions and ages, national and local governments paid increasing attention to the problems and attempted to improve local community's access to information and network related facilities. The movement toward community access points in Europe and other countries reflected the social change into the information and knowledge society. The local competitiveness in such a rapidly changing society was not possible without catching up with the change of ICT.

The development of the ICT and increase in the digital divide drove local communities to adopt the concept of community access points (Seo, 2003). The idea of community access points implies that local communities like urban ones should be given equal opportunity to access the information and network. Furthermore, it was expected that local communities and citizens could get more diverse services in real time and participate in local administration and policy through the on-line system. The term of community access point was used in different ways including electronic villages, telecottages and telecenters in the U.S., European countries and Austrailia (Kim, 2001). In the case of Korea, the term of information villages represented the government efforts to bridge the digital divide as well as to enhance local competitiveness for the rural communities.

This study intends to explore the experiences and lessons of information villages in Korea. In particular, it focuses on the institutional efforts to build up information villages and their effects on local communities. The information village project in Korea was nominated the winner of '2011 UN Public Service Awards'. About 3000 people from 122 countries worldwide visited and observed the information villages to learn the experiences and lessons of its processes and policies (Nam, 2014: 147). In a broader sense, the Korean case of information villages in particular and ICT in general would provide useful insight to other countries for a transformation into an information society, as Akhtar, United Nations Under-Secretary-General and Executive Secretary of the Economic and Social Commission for Asia and the Pacific (ESCAP), said, "The Republic of Korea's unique development experience will continue to be a valuable lesson for other countries in the region, particularly in the areas of ICT..." (UN ESCAP, 2014).

The primary objectives of information village in Korea were expanded from bridging the digital divide to revitalization of local communities and improvement of the living standards through informatization of local communities. The candidate villages were first identified and recommended by local governments, and then evaluated by the central government or Ministry of Government Administration and Home Affairs (MOGAHA), which finally designated the information villages.

The following section discusses the inception and development of information villages. It outlines a short background or context of the initiation of information villages in Korea. Definition and purposes of information villages will then be discussed in the same section. The third section delineates processes and support for information village. The fourth section reports the current state and performances of information villages. Discussions including the future challenges are provided in the fifth section. The final section concludes with a summary of the study and major lessons drawn from the case of information villages in Korea.

2. The Inception and Development of Information Village

1) Context of Information Villages in Korea

The initial efforts of information village projects in Korea were made in 2001 by the central government or MOGAHA. Prior to 2001, several government agencies including ministries at the national level and local governments attempted to bridge the digital divide and improve the local economy by adopting the ICT driven development strategies. For instance, some local governments adopted and operated 'Community Information Center' and 'Cyber-town'. However, those local efforts were so unsystematic and poorly organized that they were evaluated to be ineffective for resolving information illiteracy and unbalanced development among regions resulting from the digital divide. Furthermore, lack of cooperation among ministries at the national level including the Ministry of Information and Communication, the Ministry of Food, Agriculture, Forestry and Fisheries, and the Ministry of Government Administration and Home Affairs resulted in overlapping of design and development of local informatization movement. Thus, the government realized the significance of comprehensive and integrated design and development of the ICT infrastructure at a local level.

Information Village originated from the pilot projects in two villages of Hwangdun and Songgye in Gangwon Province, which the central government set up in cooperation with local governments and private enterprises (Seo and Lim, 2011: 95). After those cases were evaluated successfully in Gangwon Province, the authority in charge of information village was streamlined into MOGAHA in order to take a more systemic approach to expand information villages nationwide. Furthermore, the Bridging Digital Divide Act in 2001 was passed and enacted in order to reduce the digital divide among regions. Under the law, the central and local governments were required to take actions to give more opportunities for local community's access to the network and information platform.

MOGAHA selected 25 villages nationwide as the pilot communities in 2001 and expanded the number of information villages in the following years.[26] Based on the implementation and evaluation of those villages' cases, MOGAHA of Government Administration and Home Affairs attempted to develop the prototype of information villages, although it would be applied to each community in consideration of its unique characteristics such as location, specialization of products, demands for information, etc. (KLID, 2013: 217).

....
26. See Table 8-2 (p.261) for detailed information of its expansion

2) Definition and Purposes of Information Village

Information Village in Korea refers to a village or community that enhances the local competitiveness and improves the living-standards through the spread of information technologies and development of information contents as well as bridging the digital divide (Jung and Son, 2007: 21).

According to MOGAHA, information villages aimed to achieve several objectives as follows:
- To bridge the digital divide and reduce computer illiteracy through information education and training
- To increase house income communitywide and promote local economic development
- To revitalize local communities and finally cultivate sustainable communities led by citizens (http://www.mogaha.go.kr/frt/sub/a06/b04/informationVillage/screen.do)

In pursuing the objectives mentioned above, MOGAHA (http://www.mogaha.go.kr/frt/sub/a06/b04/informationVillage/screen.do) addressed physical infrastructures as well as training and education. The information village project includes several programs as follows:

- Distribution of personal computer at individual houses
- Financial assistance
- Training and education programs for computer literacy
- Development of contents for communities, products, communications, etc
- Installation of high-speed internet

• Village Informatization Centers

The purposes and programs mentioned above provided several venues to deal with education, citizen participation, digital divide, local income, and revitalization of the local community.

First, it supported a user friendly information environment for the rural communities dominated by an agriculture and fishing economy. Education and training of information and network would enhance the use of digital devices and help bridge the digital divide between the urban and rural areas.

Second, information villages aimed to establish self-supporting and sustainable communities. E-commerce would help those communities promote marketing and direct connection to consumers, which were expected to increase income and continue sustainable local economic growth. It would ultimately enhance the competitiveness of local communities by catching-up with the information technologies.

Third, information villages were supposed to operate through citizen participation. The steering committee consisting of citizens' representatives would provide inputs for community homepages, discuss the candidate projects for profits and make important decision-making for community development.

3. Processes and Support for Information Villages

The central government or MOGAHA in cooperation with local governments played a leading role for designing and implementing the information village projects. This section introduced the general selection processes of information villages, government support, related institutions, and roles of local government and villagers.

1) Overview of Processes

MOGAHA was prepared for the annual plan that included guidelines for application, timeline, the approximate numbers of the new information villages, and the size and distribution of financial assistance in a given year. Local governments that were interested in and had the potential for information village were prepared for proposals in cooperation with the village members. MOGAHA evaluated the proposals and selected the candidate communities on a competitive basis.

MOGAHA put a somewhat different emphasis on the selection criteria of information villages depending on the year. The guidelines for applications between 2001 and 2002 presented the significance of a community's willingness to transform into a information village, generation of new income through e-commerce, and unique projects reflecting community characteristics and competitiveness. However, later on, it added and addressed the significance of the balanced national development for which the candidate villages were required to diversify the existing products and businesses in order to be selected.

2) Financial Support

The annual plan for information villages included the guidance for financial assistance and its allocation for diverse programs. That is, the guidance provided information about the total amount of financial support and specific categories for expenditures.

Table 8-1. Categorical Expenses for Information Villages

(Unit: million won)

Category	Total	Construction of contents (Village level)	Environment for Information utilization		PC*	Construction and maintenance of central system	Supervision of contents
			Informatization Center	PC*			
Individual Village	180	80	50	50	local		
Seventy Villages	17,500	5,600 (central)	3,500 (central)	3,500 (local)	-	4,800 (central)	100 (central)

The Table 8-1 below illustrates the financial support and specific categories for expenditure in the year 2004. MOGAHA (2004) assigned a total budget of 17.5 million won for the new set-up of information villages. The total budget was shared by the central and local governments. The former contributed about 14 billion won,[27] while the remaining portion or 3.5 billion won was contributed by local governments. MOGAHA conditioned that local governments should bear financial burden for distribution of personal computers to each house, which was excluded from the local share of the total budget or 3.5 billion won. Furthermore, MOGAGA provided specific guidelines to local governments and candidate villages in allocating financial resources. First, expenses for construction of information contents at the village level should be allocated from the central government budget. Second, Village Informatization Centers should be supported by an equal contribution from central and local governments (or budget). Third, personal computers should be provided to each house by the local governments' budget. Fourth, expense for construction and maintenance of the central system that was around 4.8 billion won was supported by MOGAHA.

....
27. Central government budget came from 'special sharing tax'.

Fifth, with regard to supervision of contents, MOGAHA allocated 100 million won. Overall, most of the expenses or 67% of government assistance was assigned to build up physical infrastructures.

3) Promotion of Information Contents

The central government realized the significance of promoting marketing and sharing of information villages and their products with consumers nationwide. In doing so, it was suggested that the websites that were integrated and streamlined by the central efforts would lead to the effective operation of the entire information villages. Several on-line websites were created through the cooperation between central and local governments and operated to promote marketing and commercial trade (KLID, 2013: 217).

- The site representing information villages: www.invil.org
- The site promoting shopping: www.invil.com
- The site for tourism: tour.invil.com

First, the website of www.invil.org was operated by the Central Association of Information Villages. This site sought to promote communication among residents in information villages as well as among those residents and consumers. The website served as the primary media for introducing information villages to the general public. It also provided the news of information villages, offered education opportunities, provided video phone call services, and updated the events going on.

Second, marketing products of information villages and promoting e-commerce was primarily done through the website of www.invil.com, which was also operated by the Central Association of Information Villages. The website served as the main venue for distribution of agricultural products, livestock products, aquatic products, and flowers/plant.

Third, the website of tour.invil.com was set up for the tours and tourists in information villages. This site intended to provide information regarding opportunities for hands-on experience in agriculture, fishing, and recreation as well as for the service of lodging.

Overall, the website of www.invil.org attempted to develop and update information contents and is linked to www.invil.com and tour.invil.com. Both websites of www.invil.com and tour.invil.com were supported by both MOGAHA and the local governments to pursue balanced development between the urban and rural regions.

4) The Central Association of Information Villages

The Central Association of Information Villages was established in 2003 to represent the information villages nationwide. The Association consisted of all information villages and aimed to promote collaboration among information villages for mutual interests and to develop communities that maintain sustainable community development (center.invil.org). By law, the major programs of the Central Association of Information Villages are categorized as bellows:

- Research and policy recommendation for better operation of information villages
- Fund-rasing and handling for self-sustaining operation of information villages
- Identification and spread for successful cases of information villages

- Promotion of communication among IV and voluntary participation of communities
- Set-up of collaborative network system in local communities
- Support for marketing of products and services
- Education and training for member communities
- Implementation of projects commissioned by MOGAHA and the KLID
- Others related to objectives of the organization (center.invil.org).

5) The Roles of Local Governments and the Steering Communities

Local governments were also required to contribute to the initial set-up of information villages through financial support and enactment of local ordinances. After MOGAHA ended support for the new-set up of information villages, local governments including provincial and local levels led the project of the information village. Local governments not only provided financial support but also awarded the best practices for information villages to encourage sustainable growth. Furthermore, diverse events to promote marketing and revitalize local communities were held by local governments in cooperation with information villages.

The steering committee in information villages also designed a community homepage to communicate and market local products through an on-line system. It was recommended that the steering committee consist of about 15 residents who would voluntarily participate in organizing the local community for economic wellbeing and creating a sense of community. It was expected to serve as the locus of community decision-making for initiating new projects and developing the information villages.

4. Current State and Performances of the IV

Over 14 years since the inception of information villages in 2001, information villages made progress for the new set-up of information villages, bridging the digital divide, and on-line sales including shopping and tourism. This section delineates the current state and performances of information villages.

1) Creation of Information Villages

As of the year of 2013, there were 359 information villages created by local communities. As mentioned before, the MOGAHA in 2001 selected 21 sites as the pilot communities for information village, while local governments selected 5 communities as information villages (see Table 8-2). It showed continuing growth till the years of 2004-2005 and experienced a sharp decline in the annual growth rate with the new set-up of information village. While the MOGAHA reduced the number of annual selection of information villages, local governments were still active in setting up new information villages by 2009. The sharp decline in the number of information villages selected by the MOGAHA seemed to be a result of the decrease in financial support from the central government. The decrease in financial support continued till 2009 and then ended the support for information villages. Since then, local governments have played the primary role for the selection of information villages. That is, the new creation of information villages was up to local governments. The statistics in 2010 and later on reflected the end of the financial support from the central government or MOGAHA.

The statistics also showed huge variations depending on geographic loca-

Table 8-2. Statistics of Set-up of Information Villages, 2011-2013

Region	Total	Set-up of Information Villages											
		2001	2002	2003	2004~5	2006	2007	2008	2009	2010	2011	2012	2013
Total	359 (110)	21 (5)	69 (3)	74 (7)	82 (16)	26 (15)	33 (23)	30 (17)	12 (12)	4 (4)	4 (4)	3 (3)	1 (1)
Seoul	0	-	-	-	-	-	-	-	-	-	-	-	-
Busan	4	-	1	2	1	-	-	-	-	-	-	-	-
Daegu	2	1	1	-	-	-	-	-	-	-	-	-	-
Incheon	0	-	-	-	-	-	-	-	-	-	-	-	-
Gwangju	4	1	1	2	-	-	-	-	-	-	-	-	-
Daejeon	0	-	-	-	-	-	-	-	-	-	-	-	-
Ulsan	0	-	-	-	-	-	-	-	-	-	-	-	-
Sejong	1	-	-	1	-	-	-	-	-	-	-	-	-
Gyeonggi	53 (28)	3 (2)	4	9 (2)	19 (12)	6 (4)	6 (4)	6 (4)	-	-	-	-	-
Gwangwon	57 (26)	3 (1)	10 (1)	9 (1)	8 (1)	9 (7)	6 (4)	4 (3)	3 (3)	2 (2)	1 (1)	1 (1)	1 (1)
Chungbuk	22 (7)	-	5	3	5	1	3 (3)	2 (1)	2 (2)	1 (1)	-	-	-
Chungnam	36 (8)	1	10	7	7	2 (1)	3 (2)	3 (2)	-	-	2 (2)	1 (1)	-
Jeonbuk	39 (10)	2	6	8	13 (3)	4 (3)	2 (1)	2 (1)	2 (2)	-	-	-	-
Jeonam	48 (14)	2	8	13 (4)	11	1	4 (3)	6 (4)	3 (3)	-	-	-	-
Gyeongbuk	47 (9)	5 (2)	14 (2)	10	10	1	3 (2)	1	-	1 (1)	1 (1)	1 (1)	-
Gyoengnam	29 (6)	2	6	7	5	1	3 (2)	3 (2)	2 (2)	-	-	-	-
Jeju	17 (2)	1	3	3	3	1	3 (2)	3	-	-	-	-	-

* **Numbers in parenthesis are information villages created by local governments**
** **Source:** KLID (2014: 577)

tions. Metropolitan governments including Seoul that had high population density and urban characteristics were less likely to establish information villages. As mentioned before, communities located in urban areas held a well-developed infrastructure of network and the ICTs and thus were excluded from the national policy of information villages. In particular, Seoul, the capital of Korea and the most highly urbanized city, had no information village. Among provincial areas Gangwondo was ranked first in the number of information villages. Gangwondo as the first province to start with the project has been active in supporting information villages (Gangwondo website, 2014).

2) Bridging Digital Divide

One of the primary objectives of information villages was to bridge the digital divide between urban and rural areas. Two measures including a personal computer per house and the ratio of internet utilization were provided to identify and evaluate the gaps in the ITC and digital divide (see Figures 8-1 and 8-2).

First, Figure 8-1 shows the statistics of personal computers per house. Prior to the set-up of information villages, the national average rate of personal computers per house was 78.5%. The bar graph showed a big difference between the national average (78.5%) and the rural communities (29.4%) with a predominantly agriculture and fishing economy. However, after the information village project was in place, the gap between that of information village and the national average has reduced by 9%. Furthermore, information villages also observed a better performance in the distribution of personal computers per house than that of the rural communities, which were 57.4% and 72.1% respectively.

Figure 8-1. Statistics of Bridging Digital Divide after Set-up of Information Village: Statistics of Personal Computer per House

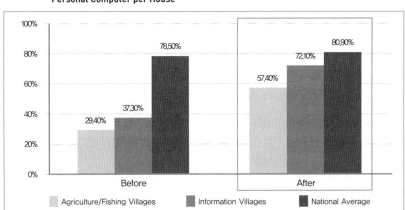

Source: adapted from KLID (2014: 153). Original source from National Information Society Agency), '08 Digital Opportunity White Paper' and Korea Internet & Security Agency, '08 Survey on the Computer and Internet Usage.

Second, the study employed the extent to which the internet was used in the comparative regions including the national average, the information villages and rural areas. Figure 8-2 shows the statistics of internet utilization per house. The national average rate of internet use per house was 59.4%. The bar graph shows a big difference between the national average (59.4%) and the rural communities (11.9%) with a predominantly agriculture and fishing economy. Furthermore, the communities that were designated as information villages later showed a lower ratio of internet utilization or 9.1% lower than the rural areas. However, after an information village was established, the gap between that of the information village and the national average has reduced from 50% to 11%. Information villages also observed the better performance in the use of personal internet than the rural areas, which was 66.5% and 35.2% respectively.

Figure 8-2. Statistics of Bridging Digital Divide after Set-up of Information Village:The Ratio of Internet Utilization

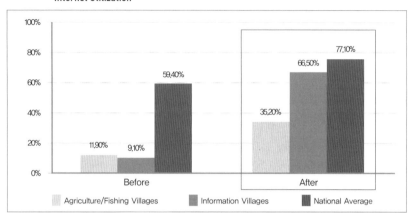

*Source: adapted from KLID (2014: 153). Original source from National Information Society Agency), '08 Digital Opportunity White Paper' and Korea Internet & Security Agency, '08 Survey on the Computer and Internet Usage.

3) On-line Sales

With regard to performances of information villages, on-line shopping through information village websites served as one of the primary venues for e-commerce. Table 8-3 below presents the total amount of annual sales in the years of 2011-2013.

Overall, the statistics showed about a 96% participation of information villages in integrated 'invil' websites (www.invil.com). Total sales between 2011 and 2013 increased by about 47.5% from 19,962,350,592 won to 29,436,423,015 won, even though there was little fluctuation in the year of 2012. On the other hand, the numbers of trade went up by about 4.3%, which was far less than the amount of total sales. Information villages located in Gangwondo and Jeolanamdo observed an increase in both total sales and trades over the years.

Table 8-3. On-line Sales through Information Village Websites of Shopping

(Unit: Won)

Year Region	2011		2012		2013	
	Sales*	# of Sales	Sales	# of Sales	Sales	# of Sales
Seoul	-	-	-	-	-	-
Busan	25,839,000	439	37,920,490	628	23,886,600	476
Daegu	51,961,700	218	10,249,560	156	4,123,030	137
Incheon	-	-	-	-	-	-
Gwangju	196,751,858	1,026	172,785,380	830	226,381,000	1,201
Daejeon	-	-	-	-	-	-
Ulsan	26,275,000	67	18,683,000	38	-	-
Sejong	-	-	-	-	-	-
Gyeonggi	1,165,057,316	9,087	2,417,410,130	7,375	2,581,274,608	9,123
Gwangwon	2,489,084,153	18,200	4,614,232,592	22,420	5,334,955,548	24,756
Chungbuk	995,631,558	6,803	2,672,599,895	7,125	1,562,829,211	6,876
Chungnam	2,247,775,857	16,185	2,309,621,935	15,426	1,493,774,828	12,192
Jeonbuk	2,645,549,534	22,273	3,229,508,046	20,745	3,133,824,053	22,728
Jeonam	3,513,603,040	32,823	6,604,637,426	32,923	9,199,653,038	43,992
Gyeongbuk	3,064,980,638	35,398	3,779,911,092	35,581	2,656,436,690	31,108
Gyoengnam	1,889,285,240	14,720	2,586,990,630	18,988	2,001,579,929	18,641
Jeju	1,650,555,698	17,460	2,483,284,757	13,946	1,217,704,480	11,033
Total	19,962,350,592	174,699	30,937,834,933	176,181	29,436,423,015	182,263

*Source: KLID (2014: 575)

4) Tourism

In the context of tourism, there is the separate website of tour.invil.com. The website was specialized for information about diverse recreation activities, hands-on experience of agriculture, lodge, etc.

Table 8-4. On-line Sales through Hands-on Experiences (tour.invil.com)

(Unit: Won)

Year / Region	2011			2012			2013		
	Sales*	# of Hands-on Experi-ences	# of Touris-ts	Sales	# of Hands-on Experi-ences	# of Touris-ts	Sales	# of Hands-on Experi-ences	# of Touris-ts
Seoul	-	-	-	-	-	-	-	-	-
Busan	74,663,000	237	4,967	20,129,510	106	327	22,690,000	185	1,312
Daegu	196,767,400	474	46,646	99,173,514	365	13,001	121,320,000	332	3,899
Incheon	-	-	-	-	-	-	-	-	-
Gwangju	29,367,000	148	3,723	19,554,000	57	2,022	38,136,000	80	3,595
Daejeon	-	-	-	-	-	-	-	-	-
Ulsan	4,680,000	13	289	-	-	-	-	-	-
Sejong	-	-	-	-	-	-	-	-	-
Gyeonggi	3,165,733,241	13,256	237,108	3,106,864,223	12,677	158,398	2,728,586,548	13,639	122,002
Gwangwon	2,071,071,390	8,690	134,106	2,806,192,643	9,438	170,699	2,492,753,905	9,649	100,769
Chungbuk	226,610,900	807	19,380	185,645,785	757	15,177	263,070,600	508	14,836
Chungnam	875,764,980	2,632	61,229	772,707,720	2,732	55,588	660,597,250	2,782	21,943
Jeonbuk	1,635,194,900	5,813	102,639	1,329,130,820	4,417	77,239	1,506,949,770	3,563	71,673
Jeonam	412,131,650	2,763	45,215	616,846,190	2,542	55,588	876,258,550	3,477	77,377
Gyeongbuk	386,936,100	2,476	27,617	441,065,198	2,520	31,436	578,570,800	2,657	36,042
Gyoengnam	983,303,210	2,282	64,288	669,950,360	2,596	55,294	633,665,700	1,876	31,527
Jeju	125,093,291	131	5,474	202,582,050	236	13,895	103,896,608	182	5,763
Total	10,187,317,062	39,722	752,681	10,269,842,013	38,443	641,717	10,026,495,731	38,930	490,738

*Source: KLID (2014: 575)

Over the last three years, the participation rate of information villages reached about 76% on average (see Table 8-4). The statistics in Table 8-4 showed a slight decrease in total sales, the number of tourists and the number of activities over three years. It implied that the decline of tourists in hands-on experience did not necessarily reflect on less interest in diverse activities. Once tourists visited information villages, they seemed to spend more money in the facilities located in information villages. However, Jeolanamdo only observed the continuing increase in all three categories. In particular, the total sales increased about 110%, while the number of tourists jumped by 71%.

The performances mentioned above were also recognized worldwide. The information village project in Korea was nominated the winner of '2011 UN Public Service Awards'. About 2,900 people from 133 countries including developing and developed countries visited information villages in Korea in order to benchmark the experiences of its processes and policies (MOGAHA website, 2014).

5. Discussions

Overall, information villages in Korea were regarded a success in bridging the digital divide between urban and rural regions. Furthermore, the Information Village project also played some roles for improvement of local economies and regeneration of local communities. The findings in this research present several factors or strategies taken by governments and local communities (Seo and Lim, 2011; Nam, 2014).

First, the initiative of IV project was primarily led by the central government or MOPAGA. The central government played the leading role for selecting the candidate villages and supporting the set-up of the system and infrastructures in information villages. Prior to recommending the candidate villages to the central government, local governments made the site selection for the IV in caution. In order to reduce the waste of public resources, it chose villages with the potential to achieve the objectives of the project.

Second, the central government established the prototype of information villages. The physical infrastructure was built up as the initial step. The central government in cooperation with local governments and businesses supported installation of high speed internet, provided are computer per house, and set-up a Village Informatization Center. In addition to the physical infrastructure, more emphasis was put on identifying and improving the information contents of information villages.

Third, while the central government established the prototype of information villages, it also attempted to accommodate the unique characteristics and demands of local communities. In other words, the information village selected had the local assets related to culture or tourism that were supposed to contribute to local development through the link with the network platform or internet infrastructure. Furthermore, the rural areas with specialization in agriculture economy were also considered top candidates for the IV projects.

Fourth, information villages were required to form and organize the institutional structure or committee to discuss and direct the project. The steering committee consisting of representatives of villagers served to organize villagers, identify and represent the community interests, and promote education and development of the information contents, and conduct decision-making for information villages.

Fifth, after information villages were in place, the local communities are fully responsible for the operation and management with continuing cooperation from governments. It emphasized the autonomy and self-sufficiency of local entities for sustainable survival of the project. In doing so, information villages also attempted to increase individual income and improve community economic conditions.

Although the government-led project of information villages was successful, several challenges still remained for sustainable development of information villages.

First, education and training should be given more attention. The development of ICTs introduced new ways of communication including social network services (SNS). Information villages got to pay continuing attention to the development of smart phone applications as well as education/training of residents.

Second, opportunities for citizens' and local participation and inputs should have been increased in the initial design of information villages. Local officials and residents felt that the central government should have taken more efforts to communicate and consult local needs and demands for better design and process With regard to participation of the committee, the steering committee consisting of representatives of residents should have been more active in promoting citizens' participation and planning the future direction regarding education, income increase, the use of information technologies for e-commerce, etc.

Third, local communities needed to take a more strategic approach in reinvesting local resources and income for the expansion of businesses and to catch up with the change of the ICTs (Nam, 2014: 159). In addition, information villages should diversify special products and hands-on experiences specialized in each community to compete with other local communities

(Nam, 2014: 159).

Fourth, the aging population not only in the rural communities but also in information villages would serve as a great challenges for sustainability of information villages. It would affect education and training of computers and networks that are crucial for bridging the digital divide and bringing innovation and diversification of local products to information villages.

Fifth, the research indicated that although e-commerce served as a platform for the improvement of local and individual income, it had somewhat limitations for integrating and invigorating local communities and sense of community values.

6. Conclusion

The information village project in Korea was one of the government's efforts or policies to enhance the local competitiveness and improve the living-standards in rural areas dominated by the agriculture and fishing economy through the spread of information technologies as well as bridging the digital divide. Prior to the creation of information villages, some efforts to improve the environment of information and network had been made by local governments, but were poorly designed and ineffective for satisfying the community's demands by reflecting community characteristics. Recognizing this, the central government or MOGAHA emphasized the necessity of a prototype of an internet platform, information contents and technology.

With this background and diagnosis of the current status of gaps in information and technology between urban and rural areas, the initial efforts or policies for information villages were primarily led by the central government or MOGAHA in cooperation with local governments in 2001. The central government addressed three primary objectives for the information village: bridging the digital divide, revitalization of local communities, and local economic development through an increase in income. In doing so, it made progress towards the ownership of personal computers, the utilization of internet (or network) for e-commerce and on-line community activities, and increases in quality of life. Furthermore, it played a positive role in the spread of villagers' mind-set for information technologies.

However, MOGAHA increasingly reduced their support and ended it in 2009. That is, the local governments took over the authority of selecting the candidate villages. At the village level, the steering committee representing villagers led the system operation. The project was ultimately aimed to empower local communities in identifying and resolving social problems through a self-sustaining system of information technology and enhancing local competitiveness.

Then, what lessons can one draw from the case of information villages in Korea?

- The central government should have a clear vision and strong will to address social problems resulting from the rapid change in the ICTs.
- The central government should take leading roles in establishing physical infrastructures through financial support and consulting. In particular, the role of the central government is critical at an earlier stage.
- Bridging the digital divide should also be linked with strategies for local economic growth such as individual and community income.
- Local communities should be able to improve management and operation of the system through citizen participation and continuing education/training.

- The set-up of an integrated website system such as www.invil.org, www.invil.com, and tour.invil.com was critical for marketing and trading for goods and services
- In the long term, the central government should turn over its leading role to the local community and thus provide the opportunity for a self-sufficient community system of the information village.

The rapidly changing environment of the ICTs would bring great challenges or opportunities into the information villages. In 2013, the Korean government announced the new vision of transformation of the government IT system into Government 3.0. It emphasized the values of 'openness, sharing, cooperation, and communication' in the government IT system, where a tailor-made IT system for individual needs and demands drew greater attention than before. This vision of Government 3.0 would be one of efforts to respond to the rapidly changing environment of mobile networks, smart phones, big data, and SNS. It is expected that Government 3.0 will also have an impact on the efforts for local informatization or Local 3.0 in terms of the spread of platforms, information contents, and citizen participation. The adaptability to such changes and development is expected to be critical for the sustainability of information villages. Some local communities might lack education and training for community members. Other communities might need fiscal resources to update personal computers and website. Therefore, collaborative efforts among governments, related NGOs, communities, and citizens are needed more than ever.

Note: This work was supported by the National Research Foundation of Korea Grant funded by the Korean Government (NRF-2013S1A3A2055108).

References

Drucker, Peter. (1999). *Management Challenges for the 21st Century*. NY: Harper Collins

Jung, Woo-yeoul & Son, Neung-su. (2007). Study of Performance Evaluation of Information Villages: Focusing on Six Villages in Gyeongbuk Regions. *Journal of Korean Association for Regional Information Society* 10(3): 19-43.

Jung, Woo-yeoul. (2003). Evaluation and Implication of E-village : In the Case of Gyeongbuk Province. *Journal of Korean Association for Local Government Studies*. 15(3): 295-311.

Kim, Gu. (2013). Re-illumination of the role of regional informatization in village: Focusing on Information Village and township enterprises. *Journal of Korean Association for Regional Information Society* 16(4): 1-26. Korean.

Kim, Seon-ki. (2001). *IT Diffusion Strategies for Bridging Interregional Digital Divide*. Seoul: Korea Research Institute for Local Administration.

Korea Local Information Research & Development Institute, KLID. (2014). 2014 Local Informatization white Paper. Seoul: Korea Local Information Research & Development Institute.

Ministry of Government Administration and Home Affairs, MOGAHA. (2014). Summary of Information Network-Village. http://www.mogaha.go.kr/frt/sub/a06/b04/informationVillage/screen.do

Ministry of Government Administration and Home Affairs. (2004). "Information Village", Emerging As a Global Model for the Information Age. Published in IT e-newsletter 4(4): 3-4.

Nam, Ki-bum. 2014. A Study of Alternatives for Job-creation through Information Village. *The Journal of Korean Policy Studies* 14(1): 147-162.

Park, Young-min. (2014). Impact of Government Policy in Rural Social Capital Formation. *Korean Public Administration Review* 48(2).

Seo, Jin-wan & Im, Jin-hyouk. (2011). Implication and Re-Evaluation of Information Village Project. *Journal of Korean Association for Regional Information Society* 14(4): 91-110.

Seo, Jin-wan. (2005). Dilemma and Search for Future Direction of the Information Village Project. *Journal of Korean Association for Policy Sciences*. 9(3): 95-114.

UN ESCAP. (2014). Leadership by Republic of Korea is key in future Asia-Pacific Sustainable Development, says UN. http://www.unescap.org/news/leadership-republic-korea-key-future-asia-pacific-sustainable-development-says-un

http://www.provin.gangwon.kr/gw/gnews/sub04_01?mode=readForm&articleSeq=2014 1203104044074

www.invil.org for the Central Association of Information Villages

www.invil.org for general information about information village

www.invil.com for shopping

tour.invil.com for tourism

List of Contributors

1. Dongsung Kong

Dongsung Kong is currently working as professor for the Graduate School of Governance, Sungkyunkwan University in Seoul, Korea. He received a Ph.D. from Arizona State University and taught at San Jose State University in USA during 1991-2005. His research areas include public budgeting & finance, performance management, and governance & national development in Asia and the Pacific. He has served as advisor to the United Nations Project Office on Governance, Mineta Transportation Institute-USA, and numerous central government ministries of Korea.

2. Cheol H. Oh

Cheol H. Oh is currently working as professor for the School of Public Administration, Soongsil University in Seoul, Korea. He received a Ph.D. from University of Illinois-Urbana and taught at Arkansas State University in USA during 1992-1996. His research areas include information policy & knowledge management, e-Government, and policy evaluation & methodology. He has served as advisor, coordinator and/or director for international and domestic organizations including the United Nations Project Office on Governance, the Asia Productivity Organization, and numerous central government ministries of Korea.

3. Eungkeol Kim

Eungkeol Kim is a director who joined the Republic of Korea's Public Procurement Service (PPS) in 2000. Since February 2014 he has been serving a three-year posting as Public Procurement Attaché at the Embassy of the Republic of Korea in the United Kingdom. Prior to this, he served as director of various divisions at the PPS, including the International Co-operation, Service Contract, and National Stockpile Divisions.

4. Yunhi Won

Yunhi Won had worked as professor for the Graduate School of Science in Taxation and is currently serving as the president of University of Seoul in Seoul, Korea. He received a Ph.D. from Ohio State University in 1991. His research areas include public budgeting & finance, taxation, and local finance. He has served as the president of Korea Institute of Public Finance, non-executive member of the Tax Tribunal, chair of Advisory Committee on Underground Economy, and advisor for numerous central government ministries of Korea.

5. Hyejung Byun

Hyejung Byun is an associate professor at the University of Seoul. She serves as a non-permanent member of the Tax Tribunal, a committee member on the National Tax Administration Reform Committee of the National Tax Service, a member of the Ministry of Strategy and Finance Tax Accountant Disciplinary Board and a council member of the Local Tax Council of the City of Seoul. She also served as a committee member on the National Tax Appeal of the National Tax Service. She is a research fellow in the Taxation Law and Policy Research Institute of Monash University. She received an LLB and an LLM from Ewha Womans University, Korea, an LLM from the University of Wisconsin and an SJD in Taxation from the University of Florida.

6. M. Jae Moon

Myungjae Moon is Underwood Distinguished Professor of Public Administration at Yonsei University. He is currently Editor-in-Chief of International Review of Public Administration (IRPA). Dr. Moon is an elected Fellow of National Academy of Public Administration (NAPA) and International Director of American Society for Public Administration.

7. Minah Kang

Minah Kang is professor at the Department of Public Administration at Ewha Womans University, Seoul, Korea. After she received Ph.D. in Health Policy Program at Harvard University, Dr. Kang has been an instructor at Harvard Medical School and an Associate Scientist at the Institute of Health Policy in Boston. Dr. Kang has published numerous articles in internationally recognized health and public policy journals including New England Journal of Medicine, Health Affairs, Asia Pacific Viewpoint, Medical Care, Health Policy, and JAMA. Her research interests are global health and governance, ODA policy, and political analysis of public policy.

8. Moon-Gi Jeong

Moon-Gi Jeong is professor in Department of Public Administration & the Graduate School of Governance and director of Sustainable Urban Development Institute at Sungkyunkwan University. He received a Ph.D from Askew School of Public Administration in Florida State University and taught at The University of Texas at San Antonio, 2004-2007. His research interests are local governance, local finance, local economic development, and sustainable development. His publications have appeared in the Public Administration Review, Urban Affairs Review, and State and Local Government Review.

The Cases of E-Governance
and Development in Korea

Publisher_ Chung Kyu Sang
Printed by_ Sungkyunkwan University Press
First Published 2015. 5

Edited by_ Dongsung Kong and Moon-Gi Jeong
Writers_ Dongsung Kong, Cheol H. Oh, Eungkeol Kim, Yunhi Won, Hyejung Byun,
M. Jae Moon, Minah Kang, Moon-Gi Jeong

Copyright © 2015 Dongsung Kong, Cheol H. Oh, Eungkeol Kim, Yunhi Won,
Hyejung Byun, M. Jae Moon, Minah Kang, Moon-Gi Jeong

ISBN 979-11-5550-110-8 93350

Sungkyunkwan University Press
25-2 Sungkyunkwan-ro, Jongno-gu
Seoul 110-745, Korea
Tel. 82-2-760-1253~4, Fax. 82-2-762-7452